Endorsements

Only Luke Laffin could ask you to *Go Face Yourself*, and you'll want to thank him when you have! His style and gift of writing will capture your heart from the start. With the mercy of the Father, Luke shares his journey and challenges us to allow God to take us higher, not with more effort, but with more love and intensity. Love from the Father and love for the Father. His deep relationship with God is imparted on every page of this book. He shares honestly and gives divinely inspired strategies that will lift you out of your brokenness and into the light and life of God. I heartily endorse his ministry. I heartily recommend his book, *Go Face Yourself*.

—Barbara J. Kohler, MS, CRC, LPC, NCC, Barbara Kohler Seminars, PLLC

Over the past several years, it has been a pleasure getting to know Luke and Helen Laffin. Luke's calm, intentional demeanor is a real reflection of the life of Christ in his life. I think he is one of those rare individuals with an intense focus to help others find their true identity and true calling in the Kingdom of God. It is evident that this flows into everything he does. He has that ability to take spiritual principles and present them in a way that is both practical and passionate.

—Dave Yarnes, Vice President of MorningStar Ministries,
President of Kingdom Business Association

Jesus told his disciples, "You will know the truth, and the truth will set you free" (John 8:32). In *Go Face Yourself*, Luke provides a wide spectrum of deep and hard-hitting truths that address some of the most common issues where we need more freedom. Written with both beauty and clarity, each chapter is sure to elevate the perspective of readers so they can see their lives with a redemptive and hope-filled perspective—just like our heavenly Father does. In addition to being a great resource for seasoned believers, this book is sure to be an important tool for discipling new believers as future decades of harvest unfold.

—Michael Fickess, Teacher and Author, MorningStar Ministries

Thank you for writing this book on how to find freedom from fear, guilt, and shame through Jesus. Only those who have experienced that freedom can truly teach, train, and equip others how to find it. Thank you for your courage to be humble and your humility to be courageous in sharing your stories and giving an outline of how to find what you and Helen have found.

— Ford Taylor, Transformational Leadership/FSH Group,
Author of *Relational Leadership*

A powerful read told with heart and story that was transformative for me personally. We all go through adversity and pain. *Go Face Yourself* is the blueprint to transform your past and present circumstances into a superpower that can change the trajectory of your life. Thank you for writing this, Luke. This is a gift and a must-read for those who want to run the race well.

—John Ramstead, Certified Leadership Coach Beyond Influence™,
Leaders Living Life Fully

As I read through this work, I was blessed by how Luke's willingness to be transparent highlights the work of the Holy Spirit. Although some things he shares may trigger emotions and memories, he doesn't leave us wrestling with them without answering the cry that arose from them. His ability to place practical instruction into easily understood language and steps will aid readers on their journey to wholeness.

—Wm J. Hurst, PhD, President of The Institute for Strategic
Christian Leadership

My wife and I have known Helen, Luke's wife, for sixteen years. When the two married, we were very aware of the hurt, pain, and torment they were going through. It is with this history that we now see two people amazingly devoted to one another and living joyfully as one. You may never read another minister's admission of his failures as clearly stated and as courageously truthful as Luke's book about how he learned to face his demons. I ardently encourage anyone who wants to overcome the pain of the past and exchange it for a delivered, redeemed, and fulfilled life full of purpose and promise to read *Go Face Yourself* and practice it as a mission to change their life for good.

—Scott Warren,
Clinical Supervisor for Chemical Dependency Treatment (Ret),
Leader of Advancement & Outreach,
Crosswinds Community Church

Go Face Yourself:
A Healing Journey

Go Face Yourself: A Healing Journey

Luke L. Laffin

Four Winds Global Foundation

ISBN: 13-978-0-9978104-3-1
ISBN: 13-978-0-9978104-2-4

Published in the United States of America by
Four Winds Global Foundation, 375 Starlight Drive, Fort Mill, SC 29715

Cover Design/ Interior Design/Production: Luke L. Laffin
Cover Graphic Production: Luke L. Laffin and Jae Gravley
Book Developmental Editing/Line Editing: AnnCastro Studio with Ann Castro
Proofreading: Jae Gravley; Scripture Fact-Checking: Katrina Ann Martin

Scripture quotations taken from the New American Standard Bible® (NASB) Copyright 1960, 1962, 1963, 1968, 1971, 1972, 1973, 1975, 1977, 1995 by The Lockman Foundation. Used by permission. www.Lockman.org

Definition excerpts from Strong's Exhaustive Concordance of the Bible. Copyright 1990 by Thomas Nelson Publishers.

Adaptation of "What is the Truth about Me?" by Neil T. Anderson. Used by permission.

Printed in the United States of America by CREATESPACE, an Amazon.com company

Go Face Yourself: A Healing Journey is an honest narrative that contains sensitive subject matter, recommended for a mature audience. This book reflects the author's recollection of events with dialogue recreated from memory. Some names, locations, and identifying characteristics have been changed to protect the privacy of those depicted.

First Edition: July 2018

To Helen...my wife, my love, my best friend.

ACKNOWLEDGMENTS

First and foremost, I want to thank my wife, Helen: Thank you for your commitment to take this journey with me and for never giving up on me. Thank you for being a student of the pain and process of healing—for loving me whether I deserved it or not. Without your love and friendship, I wouldn't be the man I am today.

To my children, Luke, Lenea, Ginez, Christopher, and Gustavo: Thank you for hanging on through the challenges we've faced as a family. Thank you for your love and support as I've failed and succeeded. Thank you for believing in me and encouraging me to be transparent about the trials we've endured. You, your spouses, and your children are my great joy.

To Ann Castro, my developmental editor and creative consultant: Thank you for the support and encouragement through this whole process. Your help in sorting through the content and structure of this manuscript has been indispensable. Without your guidance and direction, this work would not be what it is today. I'm eternally grateful.

To the AnnCastro Studio team who joined Ann on various phases of my book project: Jae Gravley (graphic production on my book cover and proofreader) and Katrina Ann Martin (scripture fact-checking). I appreciate your professionalism and attention to detail.

CONTENTS

Introduction

A tremendous strength comes from looking beyond pain and adversity into the realm of heaven—seeing God's hand in the events and circumstances of your life.

Yet in today's culture, most of us do just the opposite. We go to great lengths to avoid pain and discomfort—severing ourselves from whatever drags us down. We count trials as the result of not working hard enough and tragedy as punishment. Sometimes, even undeserved punishment. Hardships become our proof of a failed, unsuccessful life.

This book sets out to debunk those cultural lies so you can be freed. It's a book of hope. It takes you on a dynamic healing process the Lord shared with me—a spiritual journey where you can identify past emotional wounds and their sources as well as religious mindsets and their strongholds, then use God's toolset for breakthrough and living in His wholeness and peace.

Throughout the book, I share the life-changing principles my wife, Helen, and I have discovered through our seasons in the furnace of affliction—God-given truths and principles that bring freedom from the pain of the past and transformation in the present.

The process isn't pretty. There are some topics—though common to the human experience—that are downright ugly and uncomfortable to look at. And the real-life examples I've shared aren't for the fainthearted. My recollection of events and dialogue are told with great transparency, touching on sensitive matters, genuine situations, and raw emotions that make *Go Face Yourself: A Healing Journey* for mature audiences.

* * *

You may find some passages awkward to read. To be honest, they were awkward to write. They were even harder to go through. From early childhood, I learned how to abuse alcohol and drugs, turning to substances to medicate my pain. Even as an adult, looking to things other than the Lord led to two divorces, the loss of my ministry, and getting into trouble with the law. Then there were the struggles I went through while in the role of pastor.

But God reached into my life and showed me where to find Him in the midst of my failures and pain and how to follow Him out of it. Along that journey, I discovered that pain, sorrow, trials, tribulation, testing, and even temptation aren't necessarily enemies. Some hardships are rooted in sin and the schemes of our enemy—the devil. Others are part of living in a fallen world with imperfect people. And others are straight from the throne room of God.

In fact, the Word of God is full of examples where life's trials aren't all negative. Joseph was rejected, beaten, enslaved, and imprisoned, but that prepared and positioned him to rule Egypt and preserve the people of God. Moses was driven from the comforts of Pharaoh's household to spend forty years as a shepherd, but that season prepared him to lead the Israelites through the wilderness. The Israelites were tested, tempted, and tried in the wilderness, but in the book of Deuteronomy, we see the Lord using that time to establish His word in their hearts and to teach them His ways.

Time and time again the same pattern emerges—God's people enduring hardship only to be launched into a destiny forged in that very furnace of affliction.

Regardless of where our hardships originate, God has shown us how to walk victoriously in the midst of them. His Word is filled with solid promises and clear direction concerning the difficult things we face.

These things I have spoken to you, so that in Me you may have peace. In the world you have tribulation, but take courage; I have overcome the world. (John 16:33)

Even though you will face difficulties, you have the promise of hope from the One who has been victorious over every challenge.

For thus says the Lord . . . "I know the plans that I have for you," declares the Lord, "plans for welfare and not for calamity to give you a future and a hope." (Jeremiah 29:11)

This is your opportunity to partner with Him on a life-transforming journey. As you **face your world**—those things that are the result of living in a fallen world—you will be ready to **face your humanity** and those things common to humankind. That will provide the foundation for you to **face yourself** and lay hold of the Father's promises and direction for your life, becoming the vessel He created you to be.

CR῾O

Your Journey Map

My wife and I can attest to the power of this journey you're about to start. We've entered into a life marked by peace, joy, and freedom from fear. And we've witnessed the same fruit growing in the lives of those we've helped.

To help you along the way, I share my healing journey experience and my wife's, with her approval, as well as those we've discipled—however, names and distinguishing characteristics were changed to protect their identity. Also, I've created a composite of related experiences from others that I've formed into fictitious characters to protect the identity of those who perpetrated traumas in their lives.

Section 1. This is where you'll lay the groundwork for your journey— gaining a deeper understanding of the why behind trials, grasping the often misunderstood nature of God, looking past the hardship and finding hope, and discovering the spiritual benefits and rewards of trials.

These five chapters explore aspects of suffering and hardship common to everyone. Within that review, there's a clear message of hope as

I present the profoundly significant outcomes you can extract from life's challenges.

Section 2. Next, you'll learn the specific and personal aspects of the human response to wounds and the pain they produce. You'll learn about a paradigm shift moving the Christian church from a social club to a spiritual hospital.

This section also dissects the complex characteristics of the wounding process and reveals the outward manifestations of the heart's hidden wounds. You'll learn about the works of the flesh—using that knowledge to fill your toolset (needed for Section 3), identify areas of your life operating out of the flesh, and gaining clues of where to look for the root source of your pain.

Section 3. Now this is where the rubber meets the road. You'll gain hands-on tools, insights, and examples to help you in your healing process. You'll explore the impact a wound has had on your life, how to walk through forgiveness, and how to identify lies and idols—and break the agreement you've made with them. The focus is on you and learning to trust again so you can begin the journey into freedom and fullness of life.

Appendix. Worksheets you can use to better examine your thoughts through your healing process.

CRRO

A Word to Nonbelievers

Although this book is written primarily to those who have faith in Jesus Christ as savior, messiah, and God's only begotten son, please don't feel excluded from the freedom offered through these chapters. There are many steps anyone can take to move forward—regardless of the belief system followed. These precious revelations are a gift for anyone willing to receive them from the God who loves humanity and sent His Son to rescue us from the power of death. With that being said, it is in and through faith in Jesus, the Anointed One sent by the Father of Love, that you will be able to experience all that is available in this book. And with that, let me share this . . .

Jesus Christ paid the ultimate price for our salvation. He endured beatings, abuse, and death on the cross to purchase us from the power of the world and the evil one. The salvation He provided is complete. It includes our mind, will, emotions and our bodies. The purpose of this book is to remove the obstacles preventing you from walking in the fullness of what our Lord and Savior purchased for us.

Each section of this book provides a backdrop for the main purpose—to provide practical insight and actionable steps so you can break free from those things that would rob you from experiencing the fullness of life bought by Jesus Christ through His death and resurrection.

CRWO

For Every Reader: Start the Journey

As you consider these introductory thoughts, I pray you are encouraged and strengthened in your most holy faith and that you find peace and solace in the reality of God's great plan for your life.

SECTION 1:

FACE YOUR WORLD

Chapter 1

Understanding Why

This first stop on your journey reveals how God's love and transformative power are working within your hardships. This overarching truth is the backdrop for navigating the challenging and unanswered questions in your heart.

It was Sunday morning, full of fresh air and a blue sky. A small group of people I'd been discipling joined my parents, my family, and me at a campground for services. The smell of the campfire, the moist grass, and the hot cup of camp-stove-brewed coffee stirred in me a deep appreciation for God's creation and the fellowship of His people.

The children ran off to the playground for some quality time with Grandpa while the adults gathered around red-and-white-checkered-clothed picnic tables. Distant sounds surrounded us: children playing, pots clattering, and fellow campers faintly chattering on their breakfast quest.

But then there was a sound I didn't expect—a silence, followed by crying that came from the playground. I got up from the table and began walking toward the playground. Grandpa was carrying my four-year-old son, Christopher, who was crying. He'd fallen off the top of the slide, headfirst. When Grandpa stretched out his arms to hand Christopher over to me, my son screamed.

As a parent, you come to know the different cries of your children. There's one that is pretty much fabricated, usually used to get a sibling in trouble. There's one that is sincere, but more related to the lack of sleep than adverse circumstances. Then there's the one that jolts from a heart of pain—whether real or perceived. But this particular cry surpassed them all. I knew something was dreadfully wrong.

When Christopher was in my arms, he winced and squealed. I could tell by the way he reacted that the pain was coming from his neck. I figured he'd broken his neck.

I dismissed myself from the group, asked someone to handle the meeting, and got in the car with my then-wife holding our son in her arms, bracing his head against her chest with one arm and holding his body to hers with the other.

Through an interesting turn of events, we ended up with a police escort to the hospital. A gurney and the emergency-room team were waiting for us. They carefully took Christopher from his mother's arms and placed him on a gurney, immobilizing his head with weighted bags.

I was hardly even aware of the doctors and nurses scurrying about, barking instructions and moving equipment into place. Everything in the room faded as I looked into my son's eyes. I'll never forget what I saw.

The doctors couldn't give him what he wanted. There was no comfort or security in the expertise of the nurses. At that moment, all Christopher wanted was to be in his daddy's arms. He looked up at me and raised his hand, reaching for me. I wanted nothing more than to hold him to my chest and comfort him. But he had to remain still. I couldn't move him.

My heart broke as I took his hand, gently pushed it back to his side, and gave the only thing I could at that moment—some assurance that everything would be all right.

"You have to hold still right now, Son." His eyes welled up with tears. Not tears of fear or even pain. They were tears from his heart . . . from feelings of betrayal and confusion. For the first time in his life, he'd come to me for comfort and security, and all I could give him were words from an arm's length away.

Even though that happened years ago, my eyes still well up as I recall the look on his face. "Please, Dad! Just hold me! I'm afraid and in pain. Why won't you hold me? Why won't you comfort me?"

"It will be all right." That was the only response he could understand. For him, it was a small, if any, consolation.

Of course looking at the situation through my eyes, it all made perfect clinical sense. Further movement could cause more damage—and in the case of a neck injury, it could even cause death. But through his eyes, it made no sense at all. The pattern he'd grown to expect was totally different. *I get hurt, I come to Dad, Dad holds me, prays for me, I go back to playing.*

But for this situation—when the pain was worse than all his prior skinned knees and stomachaches, when he needed Dad the most—the question he struggled with was, *why won't he help me, hold me, comfort me?*

Thankfully, a short time later, our fears were allayed via an x-ray. There was a broken bone—but it was the collarbone, not the neck. Painful, but not life-threatening.

Even though it was a brief moment in the span of my life, that picture has remained vivid and profoundly significant to me to this day. In that moment and the moments that followed, I've realized I am that boy on the gurney.

So many times I've cried out to the Lord from the midst of my pain and heartache, wanting nothing more than His comfort, nothing more than to feel His loving arms around me, nothing more than to be safe. In those times I'm confused and don't understand why things are the way they are, wondering why God doesn't make the pain go away. And most importantly, why does He feel so far away?

Up to that point, I'd seen the world through the eyes of a child. But in that emergency room, perhaps for the first time, I saw the boy from the eyes of the Father. As a dad, there was no anger in my actions, no rejection, no disappointment. My only motive was concern for my child. In all honesty, I probably wanted him in my arms more than he wanted to be there, but because of my knowledge of his medical situation, I knew he was right where he needed to be.

As I contemplated the pain in my own heart for my son, the love and compassion I'd felt in that moment, I began to realize my Father was more concerned about me and my well-being than I was or even could be. It's His love alone that has kept Him from scooping me up into His arms, where He longs for me to be when I am in pain.

Not only was I keenly aware of the presence of my love and concern for my son, I was also aware of what wasn't there. I wasn't angry because he'd fallen, nor was I concerned about the hospital bill or what it would cost me to see him restored to health.

CR⊗

God and You

The first step in growing through pain and struggles is to realize that God—absolutely without question—adores you. He's not angry with you or frustrated or disappointed. He already received the hospital bill. The cost was His only begotten Son, who paid the bill in full. The Father's motive for the things He does—and in some cases, doesn't do—in your life is purely and simply that He loves you.

The truth is that the Father has examined your entire life from the view of eternity and is aware of everything you've ever done or will do. From out of the span of your life, He's chosen the moment when you were at your absolute worst to give you His absolute best—His Son, Jesus Christ. He's done this to demonstrate once and for all that He loves you.

To find the truth behind the veil of your circumstances, ponder this question: If God has proven His love by giving you His best when you were at your worst, how much more does He want to give you all the blessings of His kingdom when you've surrendered your life to Him?

To accept this truth is to forever destroy the lie that the painful circumstances in your life are there because God is angry or disappointed with you.

Like that child on the gurney, there is much you and I don't know, much we don't understand, and much we can't even comprehend. Yet, the truth we must understand and hold on to is that God's work in our lives is always guided by His love. As children of God, no matter what our circumstances may be, we have His word that He loves us and everything will be all right in Him.

That truth is simple—yet paramount to everything else in this book. Without that one revelation, nothing else will stand.

The reality of God's love for us is the only foundation that will never be shaken. It is the only foundation for building our lives. It is the only place of true healing and lasting freedom.

As unmistakable as this message is throughout Scripture, it boggles my mind to think how much we struggle to accept it as being true. I've lost count of how many times I've heard people point to the hardship in their lives and associate it with God's punishment. Whether it's punishment for doing something bad or not being good enough, the bottom line is that we feel God is angry and disappointed with us. We get lost in this endless destructive cycle filled with pain and guilt that repels us from the only source of hope there is because we think He is angry.

Our friends, family, fellow Christians, and even well-meaning ministers have used Scripture to show us how bad we are. We see examples throughout the Word of how God dealt with people who sinned—it wasn't pretty. We see a clear picture of God's anger toward sin and then we see that very sin in ourselves.

So why wouldn't He be angry with us? Why wouldn't He punish us? I'll tell you why: All of God's anger for sin was poured out on Jesus Christ on the cross. All the punishment you and I deserve has already been dealt with—it was poured on our Savior, God's own Son. For those putting their faith and lives in the work on the cross, they are in Christ. If you're a believer, you are in Christ. The penalty for sin has already been satisfied in Him.

When Jesus declared, "It is finished," He was talking about two things. One was paying for our sin, and the other was fulfilling the righteous requirements of the Law. At that moment, you and I and all in Christ were washed from our sin and declared righteous.

CRBO

God's Plan

Now let's carry that thought one step further: If your sin has been paid for and you're already declared right in the sight of God, then why are you going through this pain in your life? Why are you facing these harsh circumstances? Why are you still struggling with things of the past? Because of what Christ did on the cross, two potential reasons can be ruled out.

1. Your hardships can't be because God is angry with you for your sin.
2. It can't be because He is disappointed that you're not good enough.

Only one answer remains: It's because God loves you. After removing the distortions of self-righteousness—which is simply the idea that your standing with God has to do with what you do and don't do—it's clear the purpose of God's hand in your life is to bring you to the place where you experience all He has for you.

God has a plan and a purpose for your life. Your Father's desire is to raise you, His son or daughter, to be like your older brother, Jesus. His plan is for you to have life, not just a mediocre life, but an abundant life. A life filled with righteousness, peace, and joy. He wants to raise you up to rule and reign with Him in His kingdom. Everything He does is with this in mind.

Your first step in walking into the fullness of His plan and purpose for your life is to lay hold of His promise that He causes all things to work together for good. Whatever process you may go through to get there, rest in the knowledge that the Father is working all things out for your benefit.

And we know that God causes all things to work together for good to those who love God, to those who are called according to His purpose. For those whom He foreknew, He also predestined to become conformed to the image of His Son, so that He would be the firstborn among many brethren. (Romans 8:28-29)

When you go to Him, giving your life as a response to His invitation, you have His sure word that He will take *all* things and work them together for good. All things include everything. Or, as one wise person put it, *all means all.* That includes your wounds, failures, sins, and weaknesses. Everything. The *good* refers to your being conformed into the image of Jesus. Regardless of the challenges of the process, know that it's working toward an amazing outcome.

It's not hard to identify with that broken child on the gurney. Although he was in pain, confused, and desperately wanting comfort, Christopher remained motionless—of course, the sand bags and three people holding him down probably had a lot to do with that.

Unlike him, when lying on my emotional gurneys, I've been known to kick and scream and get mad at my Father as well as anyone else close by. I'm sure it wouldn't surprise you to learn that whenever I took that approach,

I ended up making things worse than they already were, causing more damage than I started with.

Even though Christopher may not have understood my response back then, there was enough evidence from how I'd shown my love in the past to keep him from panicking. Pain and uncertainty overshadowed him, yet there was enough trust to keep him holding on to my hand and looking into my eyes. How much more do you and I have to hold on to than the flailing attempts of an earthly dad trying to be a good father?

No matter what your current circumstances may be and no matter how confused you might feel, rest assured that you have an eternal anchor through God's demonstrated love in the gift of His Son. From that place of refuge—even without understanding your current circumstances—you can forever declare, "I know that I know my Father loves me and has good things in store for me."

You can stand with the Lord's servant Job and further declare, "Though He slay me, yet will I trust Him."

∞

Next Up

In the following chapters, we'll look at various truths, principles, and biblical examples of how God works in your life through circumstances, pain, trials. My prayer is that you'll find practical ways to partner with the work the Lord is doing in your life. My hope is that through these insights, the schemes of the enemy will be thwarted, your seasons in the desert will be shortened, and you will walk in greater freedom and fruitfulness than ever before.

I believe the Lord will give some wisdom and insight into where you've been, where you are, and where He is going to bring you. But the reality is that not all your questions will be answered and not everything you are going through—or have gone through—will make sense. Regardless of the questions and uncertainties, allow this truth to rise up in your heart: God loves you and He is for you.

Realize that even though you may be in pain, even though you may be confused and feel like God has you at arm's length right now, even though there may be many things that just don't make sense, you can trust in the Father's love. You can trust that the Father knows what you're going through. He sees the wounds you can't see. He knows the process you need to go through and what needs to take place in you so you can grow into the son or daughter He created you to be—so you can enter into the health and wholeness He has for you.

CR80

Please Consider Praying

Father, thank you for demonstrating once and for all how much you love me when you gave your Son to die for my sin and make me righteous. I confess my sin of doubting your love for me. I agree with the truth that you will never leave me or forsake me. I believe your Word that promises me that you'll cause all things to work together for good in my life, for I do love you and am called according to your purposes. Help me to cooperate with the work of your precious Holy Spirit in making me into the person you've created me to be. In Jesus Christ's name. Amen.

Now that you know that the overriding answer to the *why* questions is rooted in God's love for you, let's dig down into some details regarding where the difficulties—common to all of us—come from.

CR80

Chapter 2

A Cosmic View of Suffering

Hardship and suffering—at least to a degree—are common to humanity. Knowing where they come from and how temporary challenges interact with your eternal identity will help you on your journey.

I've always been curious and inquisitive. Once back in 1990, I lifted a barrage of questions toward heaven. But remembering what some religious folks had said about questioning God—we shouldn't ask God why things happened, just have faith—I stopped and asked Him yet another question: "Lord, do you mind my having so many questions?"

I heard him say, "You can ask as many questions as you'd like as long as your obedience to me is not affected when I don't answer."

I submit that asking *why hardship?* is the right question. Yet too often when we ask that and similar questions, we're not seeking answers—we're declaring indictments against God. That's because pain has a profound ability to skew the perceptions of life, love, and even our view of God.

- Why me?
- What did I do to deserve this?
- Why does this keep happening to me?
- Why did God allow this to happen?

But I've learned that when I actually started asking these questions with a sincere heart to understand, the Lord began to answer them. That doesn't mean I've received answers to all my questions, but I have received some. When I don't receive an answer, I've learned to trust Him in the silence. I hold the notion that the best place to start the pursuit of freedom is to ask the question with the hope of receiving an answer.

That also means being ready to embrace the simple facts surrounding the *why hardship?* question. Because if we don't, there's a tendency to bend and adjust the dimensions of the issue to the confines of our own experience. The key is to detach from that personal experience for a moment and look from above to see how hardship and suffering play a role in this world.

*My people are **destroyed** for lack of knowledge.* (Hosea 4:6)

Without an understanding regarding tribulations, the enemy will attempt to twist your perception to cause destruction. If allowed, he'll use your circumstances to sow seeds of **doubt and distrust**. He seeks to **drive a wedge** between you, the Lord, and the people in your lives.

The understanding I've received has empowered me to find the resolve to endure and strengthened me against the attacks of our cosmic nemesis, the devil and his ilk. The enemy will most assuredly take advantage of any lack of understanding regarding trials and tribulations. His tactic is to cause confusion and render believers ineffective in their identity. His goal is to bring a rift between the Lord and His people. His desire is to cause doubt regarding the heart and intention of the Father toward His children.

I am not suggesting you'll understand everything—but if you understand the overriding truths and principles regarding hardship, they'll carry you through adversity without destroying your faith. In fact, trials can become the building blocks of faith and the stepping-stones of growth in Christ. Without that knowledge and understanding, you'll be at risk.

Therefore My people go into exile for their lack of knowledge; And their honorable men are famished, and their multitude is parched with thirst. (Isaiah 5:13)

The context of this verse refers to lacking knowledge of God. In order to accurately process events and circumstances, you must have an understanding of the Lord's character and nature. Without the revelation that God is good, filled with loving-kindness and driven by His love, you won't be able to interpret the challenges you'll face in this world.

My lack of understanding led to . . .

- Being angry with God—doubting/distrusting His love
- Displaying anger toward people—blame
- Thinking I need to try harder—guilt, like I don't measure up
- Hopelessness
- Wanting to give up

In Matthew 24, it states "many will fall away" and "most people's love will grow cold" because of the increased lawlessness in the world.

As I have wept and prayed about this passage of Scripture, I've realized people will turn away from the Lord because they don't understand why they're facing difficulties. There is a pervasive, but false, teaching in much of the Western church that suggests any trials, tribulations, or challenges we face are from the devil. We're led to believe that if we're walking rightly before the Lord, the path of our lives should be easy. This false teaching is responsible for the hardness of heart in many people.

CR∞

Where Hardships Come From

Along with asking why, it's also helpful to understand where suffering originates. Understanding the sources of pain and struggles will add light to the reasons for suffering. The following subjects examine the origins of hardship—and help bring answers to the why so you'll know how to respond.

A Fallen World

Our experience in this season of creation contains various environmental exposures that are common to everyone. Whether we know God or not, we're all subject to some things because we are part of the world's current state. As Jesus states in the Sermon on the Mount . . .

For He causes His sun to rise on the evil and the good, and sends rain on the righteous and the unrighteous. (Matthew 5:45b)

Genesis reveals God's conversation with Adam and Eve after they chose to disobey Him and ate the fruit from the Tree of the Knowledge of Good and Evil.

Then to Adam He said, "Because you have listened to the voice of your wife, and have eaten from the tree about which I commanded you, saying, 'You shall not eat from it'; cursed is the ground because of you; in toil you will eat of it all the days of your life. Both thorns and thistles it shall grow for you; and you will eat the plants of the field; by the sweat of your face you will eat bread, till you return to the ground, because from it you were taken; for you are dust, and to dust you shall return. (Genesis 3:17-19)

As a result of their disobedience, this world became subject to the control of the devil and became cursed. Because we live in a fallen world, we're all subject, at least for the time being, to the negative effects of that curse. Things such as sickness, disease, pain, and sorrow are natural experiences shared by all humanity.

Our Carnal Nature

Connected to the fallen nature of man inherited from the First Adam, our flesh is a great source of trials. It is also known as our carnal nature and is part of who we are. Sadly, that part of us is unredeemable and must be dealt with in a conflict that will be present until Jesus comes or takes us home. The Apostle Paul addresses this in Romans:

For those who are according to the flesh set their minds on the things of the flesh, but those who are according to the Spirit, the things of the Spirit. For the mind set on the flesh is death, but the mind set on the Spirit is life and peace, because the mind set on the flesh is hostile toward God; for it does not subject itself to the law of God, for it is not even able to do so, and those who are in the flesh cannot please God. (Romans 8:5-8)

Throughout God's Word we see our flesh not only wages war against God's work in our life, but produces a byproduct that releases corruption and increases the difficulty of our time here on this earth.

Do not be deceived, God is not mocked; for whatever a man sows, this he will also reap. For the one who sows to his own flesh will from the flesh reap corruption, but the one who sows to the Spirit will from the Spirit reap eternal life. (Galatians 6:7-8)

Our flesh is always ready to participate in whatever produces death in our lives. Until we learn how to live under the direction of the Holy Spirit, the carnal nature will sow seeds that contribute to the challenges we face.

Let no one say when he is tempted, "I am being tempted by God"; for God cannot be tempted by evil, and He Himself does not tempt anyone. But each one is tempted when he is carried away and enticed by his own lust. Then when lust has conceived, it gives birth to sin; and when sin is accomplished, it brings forth death. (James 1:13-15)

The carnal nature can even put an unhealthy focus on things that are good and turn them into a source of hardship.

If we have food and covering, with these we shall be content. But those who want to get rich fall into temptation and a snare and many foolish and harmful desires which plunge men into ruin and destruction. For the love of money is a root of all sorts of evil, and some by longing for it have wandered away from the faith and pierced themselves with many griefs. (1 Timothy 6:8-10)

I've chosen several biblical examples of how our flesh can and will be a source of hardship and trial, but if you spend any amount of time in God's Word, you'll find many more instances of the same.

It's important to recognize that some—in fact, many—of the difficulties we face in life are simply a result of our own doing. If we don't, we'll have a propensity to shift the blame to sources outside of our control. As difficult as it may be to take responsibility for our hardship in those cases, the revelation carries with it the power to change our circumstances.

For example, if I keep experiencing pain whenever I stick my hand on a hot stove, I can get mad and blame the stove manufacturer. Or, I can take responsibility for my actions and stop putting my hand on the hot stove.

In Section 2, I'll unpack the dynamics of the troubles we cause ourselves, along with tools to help us stop doing it.

The Carnal Nature of Others

This one source of pain probably accounts for more than all the other sources combined. Even though our own sinful nature is responsible for the perpetuity of our hardships, most often it's the pain caused by others that's the origin of our greatest heartaches. Without exception, the people my wife and I have walked with through the process of dismantling destructive thought patterns and behaviors have traced their pain back to a wound caused by another human being.

An unmet need, a word spoken in anger, abusive actions of those we trusted, crimes perpetrated by complete strangers—these are the sources of pain. These are things that have happened to us through no fault of our own.

The Enemy of Our Souls

We do have a spiritual enemy. We're engaged in a battle with a kingdom that operates outside the realm of light. It's a kingdom of darkness, pain, and suffering. It's a kingdom populated by beings dedicated to our destruction.

Be of sober spirit, be on the alert. Your adversary, the devil, prowls around like a roaring lion, seeking someone to devour (1 Peter 5:8).

Finally, be strong in the Lord and in the strength of His might. Put on the full armor of God, so that you will be able to stand firm against the schemes of the devil. For our struggle is not against flesh and blood, but against the rulers, against the powers, against the world forces of this darkness, against the spiritual forces of wickedness in the heavenly places. (Ephesians 6:10-12)

Even though the carnal nature of others may wound us, it's clear that people aren't our enemy. We may be wounded by them, but our fight is not against the flesh—not our flesh or the perpetrator's. No, the struggle, the source of our hardship, is in the spiritual realm and against the forces of darkness. That is our enemy.

From God

Okay, here is a tough one for some folks. The reality is that there are times when God will be the author of trials, pains, and tribulations. In Job, God claimed responsibility for Job's suffering.

The Lord said to Satan, "Have you considered My servant Job? For there is no one like him on the earth, a blameless and upright man fearing God and turning away from evil. And he still holds fast his integrity, although you incited Me against him to ruin him without cause." (Job 2:3)

In Romans 9-11, Paul discusses both the Lord's kindness and His severity. God raises Pharaoh and hardens his heart so that He could display His glory through the plagues. Then in Psalm 78, God deals with the Israelites, bringing them into a longer time in the wilderness—and in response to their grumbling and complaining, He allows some to die. Numbers 16 tells the fate of those who rebelled against Moses: They're swallowed up by the earth. In Revelation, the Lord pours out calamity on those who refuse to repent.

There are many examples throughout the scriptures clearly indicating that God is at times the source of trials and tribulations—as well as judgment and retribution.

Your next step is learning how to use this information as a backdrop for your healing.

CR80

Now What?

As you can see, your trials and tribulations can come from any number of sources. Understanding the source of your pain is critical in identifying the proper steps to move through it and beyond. For example, if your source of pain is from your own behavior, then you'll deal with that differently than if it was simply a result of living in a fallen world.

It's important to regularly refer back to this overriding, foundational truth: Regardless of the questions and complexities you may have when dealing with pain, God loves you.

I don't pretend to understand why things happen the way they do or the full measure of why God allows or, in some cases, causes hardship. Whatever my level of understanding, I trust in the eternal demonstration of love the Father has given in sending His Son to redeem fallen humanity. I may not be able to understand the whys, but I know the One who holds my life in His hands loves me. I may not be able to see past the pain of the moment, but the One who directs my steps has my best interest at heart.

This may sound strange, but sometimes not knowing is exactly what you and I need.

There are many promises associated with the trials, tribulations, and suffering we encounter. God gave them because we need them to overcome the challenges we face. He may not always explain the process, but He absolutely guarantees the outcome.

Interacting with Eternity

No matter the source of our trials, they can work to our benefit and give us an advantage during our time on earth. Not only that, our suffering is connected to the part of us existing in eternity. It's the part of our temporary, earthly experience that entwines with the Eternal God who indwells us.

We're unable to comprehend the full measure of our current participation in the Spirit of the living God. However, our lack of understanding doesn't change the fact that we're one with Him. Our life on this planet is sending shock waves throughout eternity and impacting the natural realm with a light that radiates from the realms of heaven.

This is especially true as both heaven and the world around us watch how we respond to trials, tribulations, and suffering. As we frame the context for understanding our hardship, consider how our lives—and more specifically, our affliction—become a divine portal to reveal eternity.

You Become What You Behold

Our natural tendency is to fight against circumstances instead of keeping our eyes on the Lord and growing through those adversities. Within each of us— at the core of our being—is the innate desire for self-preservation. Our instinct tells us to protect ourselves and stay alive. This instinct compels us to increase awareness of self and of how the world can impact our existence.

The problem is that the natural tendency keeps the focus on the flesh and does nothing to bring about lasting change. That's why when you seek to save your life, you end up losing it. But when you lose your life for Jesus' sake and the good news, you find it. If you die to your natural proclivity to focus on self and instead focus on the life of Christ in you—allowing it to work through you—your circumstances are transformed into the building blocks of faith.

Now the Lord is the Spirit, and where the Spirit of the Lord is, there is liberty. But we all with unveiled faces, beholding as in a mirror the glory of the Lord, are being transformed into the same image from glory to glory, just as from the Lord, the Spirit. (2 Corinthians 3:17-18)

Who do you see when you look in the mirror? When I look in the mirror, I see myself. I'm pretty sure it's the same with you. Your mirror, your reflection.

But who do you see when you look into the mirror mentioned in that 2 Corinthian passage? According to the Word, you and I behold the glory of the Lord. When our face is unveiled by the Spirit of the Lord, we begin to see Jesus Christ's reflection in our reflection.

If we behold Christ and His nature in us, we'll be transformed into all He has created us to be. Our focus determines our future. Apart from the influence of our circumstances, we determine our destination by fixing our eyes, not on where we are, but on where we want to be.

So make the most of every trial. Understand that those trials have now been redeemed and empowered to be a force for transformation.

After the Apostle Paul is stoned—presumably to death—and dragged out of the city, he gets back up and continues to spread the gospel.

After they had preached the gospel to that city and had made many disciples, they returned to Lystra, Iconium, and Antioch, strengthening the souls of the disciples, encouraging them to continue in the faith, and saying "Through many tribulations we must enter the kingdom of God." (Acts 14:21-22)

Paul views his circumstances as a necessary part of the process of entering the Kingdom of God.

Therefore, since Christ has suffered in the flesh, arm yourselves also with the same purpose, because he who has suffered in the flesh has ceased from sin, so as to live the rest of the time in the flesh no longer for the lusts of men, but for the will of God. (1 Peter 4:1-2)

Know that in the hands of the enemy, trials are designed to destroy you. But in the hands of the Lord, they are tools that reveal your true identity and conform you to the image of Christ. Each tribulation you go through is bringing you one step closer to the fullness of God in your life.

Now let's take what you've just learned and cross the threshold of your heart onward to the journey that lies before you.

CRSO

Chapter 3

Revealing the Nature of God

Reforming your perspective of hardship and suffering will position you to understand how difficulties are an intentional component in your life as a believer. God will use them to reveal His nature in you, to you, and through you.

What did the grape say when it got run over by a car? Nothing, it just let out a little wine (whine).

Okay, I admit that was cheesy, but it does illustrate a powerful truth. When we're squeezed, whatever is inside of us will come out. If we're filled with the Spirit, trials and pressures will help release what's hidden within us.

But we have this treasure in earthen vessels, so that the surpassing greatness of the power will be of God and not from ourselves; we are afflicted in every way, but not crushed; perplexed, but not despairing; persecuted, but not forsaken; struck down, but not destroyed; always carrying about in the body the dying of Jesus, so that the life of Jesus also may be manifested in our body. (2 Corinthians 4:7-10)

Even through the weak nature of our earthen vessels, God will reveal His glory through our lives. This passage isn't a call to performance—it's a promise that reveals our Father's foreknowledge of our earthly condition and guarantees He'll still show Himself strong in and through our lives. At the end of the day, everyone will know the power comes from Him and not from us.

In 2 Corinthians, Paul outlines some pretty challenging dynamics regarding his experience and ours. There is a perpetual process of death in our existence here on earth. This death is so the life of Jesus Christ may be revealed to those around us.

CR&O

My Story

In 2011, the Lord called my wife, Helen, and me into an extended period resting in Him. He had us spend hours each day sitting in His presence in our prayer room. Often, the time we spent with Him would be filled with silence as we obeyed His instruction to "be still and know that I am God."

After our time with the Lord, we'd share our hearts and compare our journal entries. Sometimes we'd find the Lord adding revelation to our conversation. Many times, the Lord would instruct us through our own mouths—as we spoke, we were hearing those instructions for the first time.

On one such occasion Helen and I were marveling at the profound sense of safety, love, and protection we'd felt. One of us asked, "How can we take this same experience from the safety of our home into a world that hates us and wants to destroy us?"

Immediately we heard the Father say, "When you are here with me, it's all about you and the love and fellowship we share. But when you leave this place, it's not about you—it's about my Son. You will be misunderstood, rejected, and mistreated, and I am okay with that, because my Son will be revealed, and there is nothing they can do to you out there that I won't heal when you come back here with me."

CR&O

His Glory

There are times when the Lord brings us through events and circumstances for the purpose of bringing glory to the Son. There are countless examples—in the scriptures, throughout history, and even in current events—of godly men and women who have endured tremendous trials and suffering that have brought glory to the Lord. There are times in our lives when we're brought into difficult circumstances so the Lord can reveal himself through us.

I want to make this clear: Not all hardships fit into this category. It's important to avoid the extremes on both sides of the subject. Not all hardships are from the Lord and neither are they all from the enemy.

As children of God, we're called to die to this world on a daily basis. Jesus instructed us to take up our cross daily and follow Him. In Paul's letters, we see over and over again the reference to the death of our flesh as a normal part of our walk with the Lord. It's through the death of our flesh that Christ is revealed in our lives. This death often comes from our response to the difficulties we face. The opposite of this death is the comfort of our flesh.

That's not a theologically difficult subject to grasp, as some might have you believe. If our flesh is always comfortable, then we can be sure we're not walking by the Spirit. But when the cry of our hearts is to live a life led by the Spirit, we can be sure the comfort of our flesh won't be a high priority.

Our trials and tribulations can and will reveal Christ through our lives. But not only this, they also will be used to conform us into the image of Christ.

CRBO

Conformed to Christ

In February 2000, my stepmother called to inform me that my father was in the hospital—his cancer had returned, and they didn't expect him to live more than a few weeks. So my three children and I left our home in Wisconsin and moved to my father's house in California. I promised my stepmother I'd stay as long as my help was needed.

Unexpectedly—and happily—my dad began to improve shortly after that and returned home. Even though he was out of the hospital, he wasn't out of the woods, and he and my stepmother needed my help. So I remained true to my word and stayed.

But it came with a price. Several months prior to our move to my father's, my first wife and I had begun divorce proceedings. My older son was 15, my daughter was 14, and my younger son was 9. As you can imagine, the turmoil in my personal life was at an all-time high.

On top of that, I'd just launched my company into a new phase. I had five employees and two investors who were personal friends. And I was trying to navigate the complexities of a growing business while working to be a good steward of the people involved.

Having to stay at my father's meant spending several months away from my company—and that contributed to its collapse. Through various circumstances that I won't go into here, all that I'd worked to build was gone. My employees were gone, all the money I'd raised was gone, and I ended up about $50,000 in the hole.

Even though I watched the collapse from a distance, I couldn't bring myself to leave my father during the most difficult battle of his life.

One day while all these things were going on, I had a conversation with my attorney. A question had surfaced during one of our meetings regarding a legal requirement I wasn't sure had been done fulfilled. I'd asked my attorney what the potential downside or consequence might be if it hadn't been done correctly. The response was, "I have seen people go to prison for two years in situations like this." (As it turns out, I hadn't done anything illegal, but I didn't find that out until later.)

I staggered into my room at my father's house and collapsed to my knees.

For the fourteen years prior to this season, I'd dedicated myself to one thing: fulfilling God's call for my life. My goal, to be the man, husband, father, and pastor for the honor and glory of my heavenly Father. Marriage, family, ministry. These were the most important things in my life. The reality that I was losing so much on so many levels—from my dad's declining health and possibly losing my children to my collapsing ministry, business, and personal relationships—fell on me like a ton of bricks.

The emotional intensity, pain, and pressure were so intense that I literally thought that the blood vessels in my brain might burst. In that moment of profound awareness, I cried out to the Lord. "Lord, do whatever you have to do to complete your work in me."

Almost immediately I heard the Lord say, "I am answering your prayer."

I was puzzled. "Lord, I don't remember asking to have my life destroyed."

"You said you wanted to be like my Son."

Then over the next several minutes, the Lord reminded me of the things Jesus had suffered. He was despised and rejected. He suffered the loss of everything, was betrayed, and abandoned by his closest friends. He was falsely accused. And when He was going through the most painful excruciating time of his life, He went through it alone.

Then the Lord showed me how the events and circumstances in my life paralleled the sufferings of Jesus. At first I resisted the notion that there could even be a comparison. I argued, "But, Lord, that can't be. Jesus was innocent and didn't deserve anything that happened to Him. Most of the things I'm going through are a result of my own sin and poor decisions."

"True. Why you are going through what you are going through is different, but what you are going through is the same." Then the Lord reminded me of a passage . . .

But whatever things were gain to me, those things I have counted as loss for the sake of Christ. More than that, I count all things to be loss in view of the surpassing value of knowing Christ Jesus my Lord, for whom I have suffered the loss of all things, and count them but rubbish so that I may gain Christ, and may be found in Him, not having a righteousness of my own derived from the Law, but that which is through faith in Christ, the righteousness which comes from God on the basis of faith, that I may know Him and the power of His resurrection and the fellowship of His sufferings, being conformed to His death; in order that I may attain to the resurrection from the dead. (Philippians 3:7-11)

That day was one of the most terrible, wonderful days in my life. For a brief moment, I had a glimpse of what my Lord Jesus suffered for me. Never before had I realized even a portion of the depth of His unsearchable love for me. But on that day, maybe for the first time, I truly tasted His love and goodness.

He was bruised for me. He was beaten for me. He was despised for me. He was rejected for me. He loves me. Not only did I begin to understand God's love for me and what He went through for me, but also what He was doing in me.

He was using the events and circumstances in my life to conform me to the image of His Son and to be conformed to His death. How amazing and wonderful is that? That the Lord would use the circumstances resulting from my sin, weakness, and failure to perfect His work in me. That He would use these things to reveal His love for me and so I might know Him.

This is where Romans 8:28-29 started to become a reality for me. In the shadow of the tragedies I was facing, I could see God working all things together for good. And I understood what the *good* was.

And we know that God causes all things to work together for good to those who love God, to those who are called according to His purpose. For those whom He foreknew, He also predestined to become conformed to the image of

His Son, so that He would be the firstborn among many brethren. (Romans 8:28-29)

The *good* that all things are working together for is the conforming of every believer to the image of the Son.

God's ultimate purpose is for each believer to become conformed to the likeness of Jesus Christ. This is the process Paul is talking about in Philippians 3.

I declare to you that God will take every event and circumstance of your life, whether good or bad, and use it to bring about transformation in your life. There is nothing in your life that is beyond the Lord's ability to redeem. In all of history, there never has been—nor ever will be—someone who is able to make a mess so big that God can't clean it up. We don't even have the capacity to cause our Father to break a sweat when transforming our absolute worst circumstance into something that will reveal His glory.

You can be utterly convinced that God will use any and every circumstance in your life to advance His purpose for your life. Without exception. Your willing participation in this transformation finds favor with your Father.

CR&O

The Favor of God

There are a number of subjects that are difficult to navigate in the church today. Suffering, especially unjust suffering, is one of them. I've considered that topic at length throughout my life and discovered the source of my greatest challenges when I try to understand it. The source of confusion is people's teachings and opinions.

When I detach myself from the feeble attempts of presumably well-intentioned people to explain and/or excuse the sufferings of this world, I find that Scripture, in and of itself, doesn't shy away from the subject, much less try to sugarcoat it.

I agree that from my now-focused, limited, temporally minded, self-centered perspective, some of these things are hard to grasp. But if I hold to two simple truths, they will navigate me through the seasons of uncertainty.

The first is that God is good. The second is that He is for me. It's through this paradigm I can accept that even though I may not be able to wrap my head around all that I go through, I have a choice in how I walk through it.

There are certain events and circumstances I'll have to walk through. I can't change that. I can however decide whether or not to fight, complain, and resist the circumstances. I can also choose to trust my Father's heart toward me and bear up under the trial with a heart of faith and worship. If I choose the latter, that finds favor with God.

For this finds favor, if for the sake of conscience toward God a person bears up under sorrows when suffering unjustly. (1 Peter 2:19)

Would it be too bold to say that we are called to suffer? Does that concept frighten you? If it does and you're still reading this—or have subsequently picked the book up after throwing it across the room—then make a note because I'll share more about that in Section 2.

Suffering is designed to be an integral part of our walk with the Lord. The concept is clearly outlined in the verses I've shared as well as in many others. Conceptually, it's irrefutable from a biblical perspective. My goal in presenting this, as well as other passages, is not to convince you of the concept of suffering, but to help you reframe the context of it in your life.

For you have been called for this purpose, since Christ also suffered for you, leaving you an example for you to follow in His steps, who committed no sin, nor was any deceit found in His mouth; and while being reviled, He did not revile in return; while suffering, He uttered no threats, but kept entrusting Himself to Him who judges righteously. (1 Peter 2:21-23)

The example we're called to follow is the one depicted in the life of our Savior.

There is a place of revelation where we trust the Father's heart even when He leads us into circumstances that are beyond our comprehension. It's a place in the midst of our trial, allowing us to stand. There, we trust our Father and hold on to the truth that He is working something greater in the midst of it.

Therefore, we do not lose heart, but though our outer man is decaying, yet our inner man is being renewed day by day. For momentary, light affliction is producing for us an eternal weight of glory far beyond all comparison. (2 Corinthians 4:16-17)

Our willingness to trust Him when we don't understand finds great favor with Him. I personally believe that He declares our testimony in the heavenly realms. This declaration brings glory to our Father.

C凶〇

Bringing Glory to God

Our testimony in the trials we endure declares the glory of Christ in heaven—as with Job and his faithfulness to God.

I believe there is a testimony in heaven regarding our lives here on earth. And I believe that testimony is evidence in a case that is being heard in the courtroom of God. The plaintiff is Jesus Christ and the defendants are the devil and his demons.

One day as I was spending some time with the Lord, I saw this scenario unfold in my imagination. I saw God on His throne. Satan was standing in front of Him. God said, "You and those who followed you stood in my presence beholding my glory, and in spite of all you knew, pride filled your heart and you rebelled."

And then I saw the Lord point His finger at me, saying, "Look at my son Luke. He has only a glimmer of revelation concerning my greatness, my power, and my glory. And yet he willingly lays his life down and trusts me in the midst of his darkness and pain. And even though he barely knows me, he is willing to die for me. Amid all the confusion and obscurity, he holds fast to a path he can barely discern. With only a fraction of understanding of my kindness and goodness, he has trusted me all these years. He and those like him will be your judges."

I don't know if such an event actually took place in heaven, but I do believe in the message that it portrays. One of the great and beautiful aspects of our trials and tribulations here is that it gives us an opportunity to have faith in our God. If we had the full revelation and understanding regarding everything we go through, there would be no need for faith and there would be no opportunity to please the Father.

Without faith, it's impossible to please Him. Every trial we face is a container. Within that container is a fragrant offering to the Lord. When we praise the Lord in spite of our circumstances, we honor Him. When we produce the fruit of thanksgiving in the midst of our lack, we bless Him. When we bless instead of curse those who hurt and mistreat us, we're like Him.

Within every trial we face is the opportunity to give something to the Lord that no one else can give. There is no sweeter fragrance in heaven than praise and thanksgiving that rises out of our tribulation. It's a sound that causes angels to gaze at us in wonder and shakes loose the prison doors of our lives.

We're in a unique time within the span of eternity. There will come a day when sorrow and mourning and all tears will pass away. For now, in this brief moment of time, we have an opportunity to glorify the Lord of heaven and bless Him in a way that not even the angels nor any being in all of creation can bless Him. Let us take every opportunity, every trial, every hardship, and make the most of it for Him.

CZ80

Making the Most of Your Trials

Regardless of the infinite number of reasons why you may be going through what you're going through—and independent of the specific outcome God is working toward—you can be sure of one thing. You are victorious and more than a conqueror. These temporary events and circumstances contain something that is beneficial to the work of Christ in your life.

There are no victories without battles. The question is, what is available to you and worth fighting for? Is a life filled with righteousness, peace, and joy worth fighting for? Is a life of love worth fighting for? Are healthy relationships with the Lord and the people in your life worth fighting for? If you have something worth fighting for, then make the most of the battle because victory is a guarantee.

But thanks be to God, who always leads us in triumph in Christ, and manifests through us the sweet aroma of the knowledge of Him in every place. For we are a fragrance of Christ to God among those who are being saved and among those who are perishing; to the one an aroma from death to death, to the other an aroma from life to life. And who is adequate for these things? (2 Corinthians 2:14-16)

Battles are temporary, yet each one is an opportunity to engage with something eternal.

So don't be discouraged at the trials, temptations, and tribulations you're facing. Face them with faith and confidence in the Lord. God is on your side, He won't give you more than you can handle, and He'll cause everything to work out for your good and His glory if you're willing and obedient. Know that His desire for you is to be conformed to the image of His Son and He'll use all your circumstances to that end.

As you trust the Lord, cooperate with the transformation process and make the most of your trials. Use them as a platform to express faith in your loving Father and glorify Him in the times of uncertainty. Allow the furnace of your affliction to accomplish every mysterious work that it can as it rests in the hands of the God who loves you.

    To do that, you'll need to know how to find hope in your trials.

C3&O

Chapter 4

Finding Hope in Hardship

Look past the trial you're facing. See what lies beyond. This is where you'll develop a mental framework that prepares you to see through challenging circumstances into the benefits they'll provide.

Back in my late 20s, I was going to Bible school, working as a youth pastor, and working full time in construction. My first wife, our three children, and I were struggling financially, relationally, and personally. It seemed like I was going from one challenge to the next. Over and over again, I'd cry out to the Lord for deliverance from my trials. He heard me and delivered me. I remember thinking how amazing it was that when times got tough, I could just cry out to the Lord to get relief.

One morning as I was spending time with the Lord, He encouraged me to read a passage in the Gospel of Mark, chapter four. As I did, I saw the account unfold in my mind.

The sun dips low on the horizon as the crowds—who previously had been listening to Jesus teaching—disperse. Small groups of people walk slowly toward the hills, moving in every direction away from the lake. Jesus turns to His disciples, his exhaustion apparent, and says, "Let's head over to the other side of the lake."

He climbs into the boat first, heading straight to the bow, and lays his head on a cushion next to the neatly folded nets. He covers himself with His cloak and closes His eyes. The disciples ready the boat, loading supplies they'd been using on the shore before getting in the boat and pushing out into the darkening Sea of Galilee. Jesus is sound asleep before the anchor is raised.

The breeze is a welcomed friend as the sails billow with the power to propel them toward the other shore. But it doesn't take long before that breezy friend turns to foe, becoming a fierce gale. Afraid of capsizing, the sails are lowered while James, John, Peter, and Andrew push pass the inexperienced disciples to take control of the increasingly dangerous situation.

"Just sit over there!" Peter barks at Matthew, pointing to an area toward the middle of the boat. "And stay out of the way." Matthew moves, but not without trouble. The waves crash into the side of the boat and knock him off balance. The lamp hanging from a post on the bow swings back and forth in the wind, waves, and rain. Like a beacon, the light flashes on the sleeping teacher in the bow.

The night is black. The wind is fierce. The waves are violent. Even the most seasoned fisherman is afraid as it becomes increasingly clear that they aren't going to survive the night. Fear and frustration finally prevail. Peter pushes his way to the front of the boat, bobbing, weaving, and stumbling. Shaking Jesus' leg, he cries out to wake the Lord. All the disciples are frustrated at His apparent lack of concern for them. First, for sending them into the storm in the middle of the night. And then, for sleeping through their hardship.

Jesus uncovers His head and quietly closes His eyes as the rain patters on His face. His countenance fills with peace as if He is waking up from a restful nap. A wave crashes against the side of the boat, sending a thick spray of water across all of them. Jesus grins as He looks around. How can He smile at a time like this?

"Jesus, don't you even care that we're dying here?" Only one says it, but their unified glares make it clear they all feel the same way. They stare at the Lord in disbelief as He slowly looks into the eyes of each of His friends.

Placing His hand on the edge of the bow He stands up, turns His face into the storm's darkness, and with a firm resolve, says, "Hush, be still."

Immediately, the wind stops and the waves dissipate into gentle ripples, then perfect calm. The silence is deafening. The disciples stand with their mouths open, looking at Jesus. The lantern is still swinging. For several minutes, the only sound is dripping water. The sense of awe and amazement well up within the disciples—what they just observed is beginning to sink in. They are about to shout in celebration, but the Lord interrupts their thoughts. "Why are you afraid? Do you still have no faith?"

They're so amazed at His power, and their boat is resting in the middle of a perfectly calm sea—a sea that had been a raging death trap only moments before. But then that amazement is confronted with a rebuke for their lack of faith.

I can only imagine how the disciples felt. Then I realized I was the disciple in the boat.

In my own storms, I've doubted the Lord and cried out for deliverance. In my storms, I too was frustrated with what I thought was the Lord's lack of involvement. I'd feel like He was sleeping and needed to be awakened to the reality of my challenges. I'd even question His love and concern for me because He not only allowed, but sent me into, the storm of my life.

I started wondering what the outcome would have been had they not woken the Lord from His sleep. I wondered why He rebuked them, what was it they missed? What was I missing?

As I reconstructed the scenario in my mind, I realized the beginning of faith was when Jesus had told them to go to the other side. His words could have carried them through the storm. That revelation—that the power of

God's Word could carry me through my storms—began a new season in my life.

The Lord has called us to walk a life of joy. An abundant life filled with love, peace, and living rightly before Him. That is the anchor we must hold on to—it's the True North of our lives. Regardless of the storms and challenges we'll face, we can rest assured that the Lord Himself will see to it that we reach the other side. We'll walk in the fullness of life that He purchased for us.

We can trust this: If He has the power to stop the storm, He has the power to see us through it.

Even though there are many things I don't understand, I do believe the Lord has given me some understanding regarding the many storms I've endured. I believe one of those reasons is you. So let me encourage you with the same encouragement the Lord gave me:

Don't let what you don't know keep you from what's available in Him.

CʒཊO

Benefits of Hardship

I've found much hope and strength considering the benefits of the trials and tribulations I've endured. Here's an instance that actually is quite gruesome in its essence, but illustrates a truth vital for us to walk in the fullness of what the Lord has called us to.

There was a man, who after cold and careful calculation, took a knife and slowly sliced open the belly of a woman whom he had restrained and subdued. After slicing the woman open, he began to cut away at her internal organs and . . .

Okay, do you have a picture in your mind? Now let me explain what I'm describing—the surgical removal of a tumor. Based on your perspective, past experience, and frame of mind, your interpretation of my description may have been accurate. Or it's possible you thought I was beginning to describe some horrific encounter of a victim and perpetrator.

Having limited details, you might have been subject to misunderstanding and misinterpreting what I was describing.

In like manner, we're at risk for misunderstanding the work of the Holy Spirit in our lives. Since we don't have all the answers—or the full context of the process of dealing with our wounds and the sin that often surrounds them—we may completely miss the reasons we're experiencing some of the dynamics in our lives. We may see a knife coming to cut away a part of our lives. But without grasping all the context of it, we won't know how to respond.

It's vital to realize from a spiritual standpoint that an unhealed wound is like a tumor. If left unchecked, it can grow into a malignant mass that will destroy the parts of the body around it. Not only will it destroy vital organs and rob the body of its functionality, it can even threaten the life of its host. But surgery is invasive and, in many cases, can be life threatening. Yet it's the only way to deal with the tumor.

What's the risk of keeping the tumor compared to the risk of having it surgically removed? On one hand, death is certain. On the other, death is a possibility, but also the only hope of living beyond the death sentence of the malignant mass.

If we view the surgery simply from the context of the potentially damaging procedure, we'd question any possible positive benefit.

Spiritual surgery comes as we apply the living and active truth of God's Word to every area of life. And, like physical surgery, if we view it outside the context of what's being accomplished, it'd leave us wondering how something so painful can be for our good.

Consider this. Regardless of how painful it is to address the wounds in your soul, a part of you will certainly die if you don't submit to the healing process. Unhealed places in the heart are malignant tumors that destroy life and rob you of the Lord's intentions for your life. Even though there may be areas the Lord will sever, you can trust that the purpose is for health and fruitfulness. The circumstances in your life, although difficult, may be the knife the Lord uses to help remove harmful things.

To face the challenges and uncertainties of this process, the best thing to do is consider the context of your life. You're in the hands of the Great Physician and His heart is to heal, deliver, and restore. He will only bring you through those things that will be beneficial to you in the end.

As you lay hold of this hope, you'll begin to discover the riches hidden within the trials you face.

❧

Chapter 5

The Benefit Factor

There is an eternal value to what is forged in the temporary fires of your trials. Understanding these benefits and rewards help you establish a secure foundation and find courage to address the personal pain in your heart.

Years ago, as a young pastor, I was frustrated by the challenges facing me. Were they from my flesh, the devil, or the Lord?

I cried, "Lord, show me where this struggle is coming from. If it's from you, I'll accept it. If it's my flesh, I'll change. If it's the devil, I'll fight against it. Show me!"

Immediately I heard in the spirit, "What does it matter where your trials come from? The only question you need to ask is *what should I do with it now that it's here?*"

I'd been so hung up on the origin that it never occurred to me it was irrelevant. The real issue was seeking the Lord on how to move forward. The enemy lost a lot of power over me that day. I began to realize that where I placed my focus was critical for receiving what the Lord had prepared for me.

There were times the Lord directed my attention to my flesh or the enemy—but only to address the dynamics of what He was working in me at the moment. And there were times He'd bring events of the past before me for healing and freedom and to help me keep my gaze forward.

It was through the simplicity of inviting the Spirit into my current circumstances that I learned to find the benefits of what I was going through.

We'll discuss that more in Section 2. But first, let's look at those benefits.

 CR&O

Benefit 1:
Teaches Us the Seriousness of Sin

Hardship that comes as a result of our own sin and disobedience to the Lord can be a great tool that builds a defense against the power of temptation.

In 2000, my father died. The following year, my divorce was finalized. Feeling lonely—and afraid of being alone—I looked for companionship.

I got to know a lady and asked the Lord about her. I heard the Lord say very clearly, "She is not your wife. Treat her as your sister." Ignoring what I'd heard, I proceeded to come up with many reasons why this woman was right for me. To make a long story short, I pressured her and rushed into marriage.

As you might easily imagine, it was a disaster. After only five months, she filed for a divorce. I was devastated. Not simply because she divorced me, but because of all the hurt and confusion I'd caused her, her children and family, my children and family, and myself. All a result of my sin. My disobedience. I can't begin to describe the pain I felt as the weight of what I'd done hit me.

The flame of affliction ravaging me was lit by my own hand. I learned about the seriousness of sin. The pain I endured proved to be a powerful motivation to flee from sin's pleasures. The scars I carry from that sin have kept me from wandering down paths that would lead me to harm. Had I not reaped the bitter harvest of my sin, I don't think I'd have realized the danger of sin to the level I do now. Nor would I have perceived the extended implications of how my sin has the power to cause pain in others.

There is no temporary sweetness worth the bitter price that's required by our sin.

Without a doubt, the Lord has used the pain and hardship I experienced to benefit me in powerful ways. It also drove me to separate myself from other things to enter a time of healing and restoration—which prepared me for the bride He had for me in 2005.

Although this is not directly relevant to the benefits of hardship, the Lord also used pain and hardship to give me a great revelation of His grace and kindness. Even though I'd rebelled against His Word and direction, He never left my side for a moment. He walked with me, step by step, through the process of repentance, healing, and restoration. He made it very clear that what I went through was not punishment from Him—it was the consequence of my actions. He didn't remove the consequence from me, but gave me His grace and walked with me through the process of working it out.

We're free from guilt and shame, but the Word is clear: We reap what we sow. This reaping is a powerful weapon in our hand that can be used to defeat the enemy. If we allow the Lord to show us, we will see the destruction our sin has caused—not only in our life, but also those around us. Armed with this revelation, we can teach and warn others with authority and compassion regarding the seriousness of sin.

Learning about the seriousness of sin doesn't have to come only from your experience. You can observe the consequences played out in the world around you on a daily basis. You can also refer to the devastation recorded in God's Word. The greatest example is the brutal beating and death of Jesus Christ. His suffering was not only a demonstration of His great love, but also of the consequence of sin.

CRSO

Benefit 2:
Disciplines Us for Sin

Discipline—it's proof of His love. Our Father uses the pain of sin to discipline us. It's not punishment for our sins. Let me explain the difference.

Punishment is the infliction or imposition of a penalty as retribution for an offense.

Since God's anger for sin was poured out on His Son, the full price for our sin has been pain. Therefore, the need for retribution was removed for those who are in Him. As believers, we are not subjected to that kind of punishment.

Discipline, on the other hand, is the application of undesirable events or circumstances to bring about a positive outcome. We can be confident that any consequence of sin we bear will have a redemptive quality to it.

Simply put, punishment looks back—discipline looks forward.

. . . and have you forgotten the exhortation which is addressed to you as sons, "My son, do not regard lightly the discipline of the Lord, Nor faint when you are reproved by Him; For those whom the Lord loves He disciplines, And He scourges every son whom He receives." (Hebrews 12:5-6)

As you and I endure this divine discipline, we need to remember that God is treating us as His own children. Who ever heard of a child never being disciplined by its father? If God didn't discipline us, it would mean we're illegitimate and not really His children at all. Since we respected our earthly fathers who disciplined us, shouldn't we all the more submit to the Father's discipline of our eternal soul?

For our earthly fathers disciplined us for a few years, doing the best they knew how. But God's discipline is always good for us so we might share in His holiness. No discipline is enjoyable while it's happening—it's painful! But afterward there will be a peaceful harvest of right living for those who are trained by it.

* * *

According to Scripture, any discipline or punishment His children endure is carefully employed by a loving Father for our benefit and success. His discipline is for *our* benefit, not His. That is to say, He is not doing it to satisfy His own need for justice or retaliation. It is so *we* may share in His holiness, which ultimately results in a life marked by righteousness, peace, and joy.

It may not feel like it at the time, but God's goal for your life is filling it with joy. Jesus made it quite clear. In fact, it was one of His primary objectives. He came so we would have an abundant life filled with joy. His discipline is designed with that outcome in mind.

It's important to always remember the focus is not on the past, but on the future.

The enemy of our souls will try to point to our past and highlight our failures and sins. If he can get us to filter our sense of worth through the past, we'll become entangled in his skillfully woven web. It's a web designed to entrap and prevent us from moving forward into God's purposes for our lives. It's a web built with the cords of guilt, shame, and regret. The cross destroyed the power of those cords. You have no obligation to accept any of them.

The past can't be changed—but if you combine it with the discipline of the Lord, it will transform your future.

CRISO

Benefit 3:
Fulfills Prayer

My first son was born shortly after my first anniversary. I was twenty-one years old, struggling in every area of my life, emotionally, relationally, financially, and spiritually.

Often I'd have outbursts of violent anger. I just couldn't control it. In my desperation, I cried out, "Lord, please give me patience!"

Immediately, a blue mist glowing with light began to descend into the room. The mist swirled and danced around my head, imparting a sweet perfume that covered my whole body in an anointing of patience. I never lost my temper again.

Wait. That wasn't what happened—that's what I thought would happen. Actually what happened was everything I was going through got worse. My son went from being fussy to extended bouts of crying. I started having car troubles. Our finances got worse. And . . . well, I think you get the idea.

It was so obvious that everything got worse after I prayed, I felt responsible to warn people not to ask God for patience. For months I told people, "Whatever you do, don't pray for patience!" It was then that I discovered I wasn't the only one who'd had this experience—and I took exception to the notion others knew this and hadn't warned me.

One day as I was spending time with the Lord, He asked me a question. "Is patience a good thing?"

I answered, "Yes, Lord."

Then He asked me another question, "Then why would you tell people not to ask me for it?"

"Well, I asked you for patience and all hell broke loose!" I said.

In that moment, I realized He was actually answering my prayer. I'd thought it would be some magical-wand request where He'd just drop a dose of patience into me. In reality, He'd heard my heart cry and answered me. He orchestrated my circumstances, gave me His grace, and then began leading me down the path that would cultivate patience within me.

There is a powerful principle depicted within this simple anecdote. It applies to many situations. And without much effort, you'll see it played out time and again in Scripture and in our lives.

Consider the Israelites. They cried out for deliverance, and the Lord led them out of Egypt to the Red Sea. They were trapped with no ability to fight or flee, then God made a way. And consider the way He led them— straight into the wilderness. He gave them a promise of entering a land flowing with milk and honey. Their first stop was at a spring with bitter waters.

I've asked for many wonderful things from the Father. I've known many brothers and sisters who have done the same. I've seen over and over again that the first step in the journey toward the answer is a season of what seems to be the exact opposite of what we asked for.

Did you ask for wealth so you could share it with the poor or to reach the lost? I did.

Here's what I thought would happen:

Knock, knock, knock.

"Who's at the door?"

"It's the Prize Patrol. Are you Mr. Luke Laffin?"

"Yes, that's me."

"You've won a million dollars!" Imagine the balloons, confetti, and music. What a celebration it would be.

But here's what really happened:

Knock, knock, knock.

"Who's at the door?"

"It's the sheriff's department. Are you Mr. Luke Laffin?"

"Yes, that's me."

"You've been evicted. You have one week to vacate the premises."

True story by the way. So what's the deal? Is God just mean or have a sadistic sense of humor? No. Emphatically, no. The real heart of the issue is trusting that God is good and knowing He has our best interest in mind regardless of how it may appear.

It's not hard to understand. To handle being a millionaire, you need to know how to manage money. That's best accomplished when you don't have enough because you're required to understand how it works and how to prioritize. It's also vital to learn to live by faith and trust in the Lord— otherwise wealth can become a terrible stumbling block and a false idol.

Jesus stated the wealthy enter the kingdom with great difficulty. That being the case, it shouldn't be a surprise to learn that the season of preparation is arduous.

I am not trying to build a case for patience or wealth. What I am stating is there is a predictable pattern that's important to identify if we're to understand the benefits of such hardships.

The pattern is this: If you make a request of your loving Father in accordance with His desire for you, He'll grant it. The next step in the process is vital for consummating the request and guaranteeing its fruition. You must know that God is good and trust Him with the process of preparing you to receive what you've requested. The secret is found in John 15.

If you abide in Me, and My words abide in you, ask whatever you wish, and it will be done for you. (John 15:7)

Here is how I understand that verse: Ask me for whatever you wish. If you're willing to obey me, trust me, remain in me while submitting yourself to the necessary process of preparation, I'll give you whatever you ask.

When we understand that our Father's heart is for us and that He truly wants to richly give us all good things to enjoy, we can trust the process we need to go through. We can trust that the challenges and hardships we endure will be used to build the character we need to handle the fulfillment of our requests. We can trust His love and His wisdom.

We may be praying for a house, but the Lord knows we need a foundation first. Abide in Him and in His Word through the season of preparation. Hardships are a part of our training—so we'll go deeper into that in Section 2.

But now, I want to expose a tactic the enemy has effectively used against believers regarding this preparation process. In fact, he's used our lack of understanding regarding this process as a tool of great destruction.

The suspicion that caused me to doubt the goodness of God when I'd asked for patience is the same suspicion the enemy has planted within the hearts of many. His lie points to the discomfort of our current circumstances and says, "See! This God you pray to doesn't care about you. As a matter of fact, He's angry that you would even ask Him for something good. He is teaching you a lesson. Don't ask Him for anything or your life will get worse."

Sometimes the enemy's lies are bold and in your face. Sometimes they're subtle hints that suggest that God doesn't really like or care about you.

I know these tactics through firsthand experience. The enemy used my circumstances in the two examples I shared—along with many others in my life—to try to sow seeds of distrust in my heart for the Lord. Ultimately, the enemy's tactics were unsuccessful with me because I refused to allow my limited understanding of my circumstances to override the promise of God's Word. The only thing the enemy was successful in accomplishing was to solidify my faith and confidence in my Father's love for me. In a very real and practical way, the hardships I've endured have trained and prepared me in ways I could never have imagined.

Fix your eyes in faith. Believe for the outcome you've asked for. If you've asked according to His will, He heard you and has granted what you've requested. Every obstacle you face in the process will prepare you for the time when your prayer is answered.

Benefit 4:
Trains Us

In Hebrews 12:11, we see the benefits of discipline and the affirmation of the love of the Father. But I want to draw attention to the fact that it contains an element of training.

All discipline for the moment seems not to be joyful, but sorrowful; yet to those who have been trained by it, afterwards it yields the peaceful fruit of righteousness. (Hebrews 12:11)

When it comes to training, there is nothing that compares to experience. In fact, even Jesus had to learn obedience by experience. Consider these passages in Hebrews.

For it was fitting for Him, for whom are all things, and through whom are all things, in bringing many sons to glory, to perfect the author of their salvation through sufferings. (Hebrews 2:10)

Although He was a Son, He learned obedience from the things which He suffered. (Hebrews 5:8)

I find this truth both amazing and comforting. Amazing from the standpoint that Jesus' human experience required the same process of maturation as mine. Even though He was the embodiment of truth, He still needed to go through the process of time and trials in order to enter into the completeness of His humanity. It's comforting from the standpoint that He can identify with my weakness and struggles—yet has proven that He has given me everything I need to succeed in who He has called me to be.

The acquisition or containment of knowledge is not the goal. We can have all knowledge and yet we still must apply that knowledge before we will come to maturity. Hardships are the opportunity to practically employ all that the Father has revealed to us.

My wife, Helen, and I were having a candid conversation a number of years ago. We were both receiving profound revelation regarding the practical nature of God's power in us to live out all that He has given us through His Son.

It was in a particular time of frustration while navigating through some of the wounds in my heart that I was expressing myself in less than congenial terms. My wife was perplexed and shook her head. "How can you have such wisdom and insight into these truths about the nature of Christ in you and yet behave this way?"

Without really even thinking about it, I said, "Just because the Lord is showing me these things doesn't mean I have all the answers. I'm in the process of figuring it out and learning how to apply it to myself, even as I'm sharing it with you."

In retrospect, I believe that was a key we both needed in that season. Yes, the Lord was revealing some amazing things. They were eternal and powerful truths. Truths that wouldn't be diminished by my failure to apply them. Truths that wouldn't be augmented by my adherence. And yet the power of these truths created a fire in my life. It was a fire that the Holy Spirit invited me to walk through so that I could learn how to apply the knowledge to my day-to-day life.

God reveals His truth with the full understanding that we won't be able to live up to it without Him. He is not surprised that we have to go through a training process in order to learn how His principles apply to our lives. He's not only aware of the process, He is okay with it. After all, it's the process He created and it's the same process His Son went through. Jesus learned obedience through the things He suffered. He was perfected, that is, brought to fullness and maturity, through the things He suffered.

Both Paul and James write about this process in their letters to the early church. Paul encourages us to "exult in our tribulations." That seems preposterous at first glance. But within the context of this passage in Romans 5, we see a beautiful description of a process that unfolds over time.

Therefore, having been justified by faith, we have peace with God through our Lord Jesus Christ, through whom also we have obtained our introduction by faith into this grace in which we stand; and we exult in hope of the glory of God. And not only this, but we also exult in our tribulations, knowing that tribulation brings about perseverance; and perseverance, proven character; and proven character, hope; and hope does not disappoint, because the love of God has been poured out within our hearts through the Holy Spirit who was given to us. (Romans 5:1-5)

There are three things that stand out to me in this passage. The first is the foundational revelation of what has been accomplished through Jesus Christ. We've been given an introduction into an immovable faith where we've already been established. From this place of security, we move into a place where we also exult in our tribulations because of what they accomplish. Thirdly, there is the hope that brings us through this process of development.

We can see that the tribulation we go through is designed to develop perseverance, to develop our character, and to bring us into a life marked by a hope—a hope that can't be disappointed because through each step of the journey, God is pouring out His love within our hearts through the Holy Spirit.

Consider it all joy, my brethren, when you encounter various trials, knowing that the testing of your faith produces endurance. And let endurance have its perfect result, so that you may be perfect and complete, lacking in nothing. (James 1:2-4)

James also clarifies that the outcome is so powerful that we can actually consider it pure joy when we encounter trials.

Ten years ago, I really struggled to grasp this in a practical way. I was able to see the value in trials and hardships, but consider them joy or exult in them? Not so much.

Five years ago I could see that I no longer had the fear or dread of facing hardships. I actually began to appreciate them because I was discovering a pattern. The Lord would bring me into events and circumstances that would expose wounds in my heart or lies that I was holding on to or other beliefs that were undermining my ability to experience His fullness in my life.

Now I can honestly say I do exult in the challenges I face and consider it joy when I am tested. I rejoice because I know when something happens that causes my flesh to rise, my Father is bringing me to a new place of healing and wholeness. **The outcry of my carnal nature is the harbinger of my freedom.**

My trials and hardships have trained me to live by the Spirit and walk in freedom from the power of the flesh. I'm still in the process and can't claim that I don't have bouts with my carnal nature. But when the battle comes, I know how to use the *weapons of righteousness for my left hand and my right hand* to protect myself on all sides as 2 Corinthians 6:7 instructs.

Along this healing journey, the same will happen for you. You'll gain training through the trials, and the Lord will also use the furnace of affliction to test and refine you in Him. This furnace is designed to melt you down like a precious metal, separating the worthless from the precious in your life.

CR80

Benefit 5:
Tests and Refines Us

Don't be surprised. God is much more concerned with our character than He is our comfort, as any good father would be.

The Bible is filled with many examples of godly men and women who have endured trials, temptations, and testing even though they didn't deserve it. In example after example, the outcome of their afflictions was a preparation for their calling and destiny.

I've met many people who have had awesome promises spoken over their lives, and yet those promises remain unfulfilled—at least for now. I'd count myself among this great company of believers. I also believe with all my heart that if you're reading this book, you are among them as well.

I am convinced of this because if you're reading this book, then you've been through the fire—and, quite possibly, are still in it. And if you're in the fire, then you're being refined and prepared for a noble purpose in the household of God.

I've often pondered the life of Joseph. As a matter of fact, he's one of the first people I want to meet. I'd like to hear about the process he endured to prepare for his role in the Father's plans and purposes.

At seventeen years old, Joseph received two dreams that revealed God's great purpose for his life. He was so excited that he told his family, but the news wasn't well received. His father, Jacob, was displeased with him, despite the fact he was the favored son.

The disappointing reaction from his family was just the beginning of a painful and progressively bleak series of events that would last until he was thirty years old. He was beaten and thrown into a pit, sold into slavery, falsely accused, then thrown into prison and forgotten. Each of the transitions in his life—from the time he received the promise—seemed to be moving him another step further away from what God had revealed to him. What was going on in his mind during that season? How did his circumstances affect his heart, his faith, his hope? We get a glimpse in Psalm 105.

He sent a man before them, Joseph, who was sold as a slave. They afflicted his feet with fetters, he himself was laid in irons; until the time that his word came to pass, the word of the Lord tested him. (Psalms 105:17-19)

The word Joseph received—that beautiful, horrible, frustrating, amazing word—tested him over and over again until the time it came to pass. The circumstances would be difficult, painful, and challenging. But the circumstances, along with a word promising an impossible outcome, created a furnace that melted Joseph over and over again. Each time the flames increased, it drove out the dross of his humanity that would have prevented him from fulfilling his unparalleled role in history.

I believe you're such a person as Joseph. The promises over your life are great and amazing and utterly impossible. Your circumstances are bleak, and there may seem to be no way to get from where you are to the pinnacle of the purpose He has declared over you. The word of promise over your life has been the source of trouble and frustration—yet it has kept you standing in the flames, refusing to abandon the destiny you know in your heart is from your Father. You have pressed in to the crucible of refining. Even though you don't understand it, you are holding on to hope. You are holding on to faith and you are being tested.

For You have tried us, O God; You have refined us as silver is refined. (Psalms 66:10)

I have great hope for you, as I do for myself, that just like Joseph, you and I will be snatched up from the fire and placed in our Father's household to fulfill our noble function. For even as gold and silver are refined to remove the dross and be made pure, so too is the Lord preparing us.

We have already obtained an inheritance in Christ that can't be taken away, but requires a refining process so we can fulfill His purpose for our lives.

Blessed be the God and Father of our Lord Jesus Christ, who according to His great mercy has caused us to be born again to a living hope through the resurrection of Jesus Christ from the dead, to an inheritance which is imperishable and undefiled and will not fade away, reserved in heaven for you, who are protected by the power of God through faith for a salvation ready to be revealed in the last time.

In this you greatly rejoice, even though now for a little while, if necessary, you have been distressed by various trials, so that the proof of your faith, being more precious than gold which is perishable, even though tested by fire, may be found to result in praise and glory and honor at the revelation of Jesus Christ; and though you have not seen Him, you love Him, and though you do not see Him now, but believe in Him, you greatly rejoice with joy inexpressible and full of glory, obtaining as the outcome of your faith the salvation of your souls. (1 Peter 1:3-9)

The trials and testing we endure are not random. They are divinely orchestrated and controlled by the Refiner. This process of refining is designed to bring about praise, glory, and honor at the revealing of Jesus Christ and be integrated into the deliverance and full application of God's provision for our souls. It's important to understand that this kind of testing and refining is part of the process the Lord has designed to bring His purposes to pass in our lives.

Beloved, do not be surprised at the fiery ordeal among you, which comes upon you for your testing, as though some strange thing were happening to you; but to the degree that you share the sufferings of Christ, keep on rejoicing, so that also at the revelation of His glory you may rejoice with exultation. (1 Peter 4:12-13)

The events and circumstances in your life as a believer—loving Him and being directed by Him—are designed by your Eternal Father to produce an effect that ultimately works toward establishing the benefits He intends. The process, however, may look very different than the outcome He is in the process of working out in you. You will need to brace yourself for the ugliness of that process.

CABO

Expect the Dross

I'm going to be completely honest with you. There have been times when the refining process of my life has been brutal. The intensity of the circumstances—combined with the revealing of what was hidden in my soul—shook me to the core.

In one particular instance, I found myself in the midst of a crucible that was causing a response in me that was nothing short of disgusting. Anger, hatred, and bitterness of soul were bubbling up in me to the point that I was questioning if I could even be saved. The ugliness of what was still inside me, even after decades of walking with the Lord and pursuing His will for my life, caused a sense of hopelessness and despair.

In the midst of seeing the intense depravity in my soul, I heard the Lord speak to me, "Son, don't forget what lies beneath the dross."

The Lord increases the intensity of the refining fire in our lives not just to reveal the dross, but to remove it.

You must hold fast to the reality that the dross of your soul doesn't belong there. The Father redeemed your soul because of the great value He placed on it. The process of refining is what the Lord uses to separate the precious from the worthless in your life.

So if you're in the midst of a trial that is revealing ugliness in your soul, know it is a cause for rejoicing and celebration. If you can see the dross, then you know that it's the time to be free from it.

In Section 3, you'll learn the practical steps needed to remove the dross. The purpose of mentioning it here is to bring understanding about the process, seeing your tests and trials for what they truly are—steps to the freedom that was purchased for you and available to you in Christ.

● ● ●

Behold, I have refined you, but not as silver; I have tested you in the furnace of affliction. (Isaiah 48:10)

છ૭ૐ

Benefit 6:
Sets the Joy before Us

Most people I've met have a pretty good grasp that it's possible to look at a difficult time in life and walk away with something positive. Pushing beyond the cliché comments given in the midst of hardship—from the emotionally detached pat on the back to buck up, hang in there, everything works for the best, or it could be worse—consider Paul's encouragement to those going through trials.

And not only this, but we also exult in our tribulations, knowing that tribulation brings about perseverance; and perseverance, proven character; and proven character, hope; and hope does not disappoint, because the love of God has been poured out within our hearts through the Holy Spirit who was given to us. (Romans 5:3-5)

Paul discovers a truth that transforms the way he views hardship. It's the revelation that tribulations can literally produce perseverance, character, and hope. James also echoes the same thought in his letter to the church.

Consider it all joy, my brethren, when you encounter various trials, knowing that the testing of your faith produces endurance. And let endurance have its perfect result, so that you may be perfect and complete, lacking nothing. (James 1:2-4)

These writers lay out several key factors in bringing this truth to light. First is the knowledge that our circumstances are producing something. Secondly, they are perfecting something.

The necessity of adversity in our lives is integrated within the foundation of our faith. Too often we come to the Lord with less than the full picture of His plan for us and through us. In a nutshell, not only are we saved *from* something, but we are also saved *for* something.

For by grace you have been saved through faith; and that not of yourselves; it is the gift of God; not as a result of works, so that no one may boast. For we are His workmanship, created in Christ Jesus for good works, which God prepared beforehand so that we would walk in them. (Ephesians 2:8-10)

We were not only saved from hell, but transferred into the Kingdom of Light where each of us has a role to play, a purpose. It's important to understand that there is a process we'll go through to prepare us for that purpose.

For I am confidant of this very thing, that He who began a work in you will perfect it until the day of Christ Jesus. (Philippians 1:6)

The Lord Himself takes responsibility to continue the work of perfecting and transforming us, using every circumstance. There is a purpose and a plan that lies at the heart of the challenges we face on our journey toward Him.

As you lay hold of these truths, you can begin to look beyond the temporal circumstances and see a greater purpose unfolding before you.

What Is the Joy before Us?

Jesus endured a level of pain, sorrow, and suffering that you and I can't comprehend. He faced the cruel and grueling ordeal of scourging and crucifixion as a man. A man subject to the same feelings, same temptations, and same weaknesses that you and I have. Hebrews gives us a clue how He was able to endure His furnace of affliction.

Therefore, since we have so great a cloud of witnesses surrounding us, let us also lay aside every encumbrance and the sin which so easily entangles us, and let us run with endurance the race that is set before us, fixing our eyes on Jesus, the author and perfecter of faith, who for the joy set before Him endured the cross, despising the shame, and has sat down at the right hand of the throne of God.

For consider Him who has endured such hostility by sinners against Himself, so that you will not grow weary and lose heart. (Hebrews 12:1-3)

The pain of the cross was directly in front of Jesus' eyes as He approached the appointed day. However, His eyes weren't fixed on the cross, but on what was beyond it. He endured the cross and despised the shame.

In the Greek, the word for *despising* means *to hold in contempt, think lightly of, despise, neglect, not to care for*. In essence, the passage states that Jesus didn't give much thought to the shame, because the joy set before Him was of much greater value.

As you walk through the pain and hardship of this world, you too can shift the value of your focus beyond how the Lord is perfecting you to the joy of what He is accomplishing in you.

CRBO

Benefit 7:
Strengthens Our Armor

Imagine a warrior on the battlefield, dressed in full armor and ready to fight—with one, small exception. He forgot to put on part of his breastplate. Where do you think his enemy will aim?

Years ago I'd get so frustrated whenever I'd keep stumbling, struggling, and falling in the same area of my life. Then the Lord showed me the picture of the warrior I just described. The problem wasn't that I kept getting attacked in the same area, the problem was that area of my life was exposed.

The bows of the mighty are shattered, But the feeble gird on strength. (1 Samuel 2:4)

I realized that the enemy wasn't my problem. In fact, he was just doing what is natural to him. The problem was an area of my heart that was out of agreement with the truth. The problem was that I had no armor protecting that part of my life.

Not only was the enemy not my problem, he actually did me a huge favor by helping me to identify an area of my belief system that was in agreement with him. When I realized this, I brought that area of my life before the Lord as part of a serious conversation regarding my thinking process.

I've come to believe that in the lives of committed believers, the enemy can only accomplish one thing—drive us closer to the Father.

If he attacks me and succeeds, then he just helped me discover a vulnerability in my life that I'll bring to the Lord.

If he tempts me and I succumb, then he just helped me identify an idol in my life that I'll destroy at the feet of my Lord.

If he trips me and causes me to stumble, then he just helped me identify the stumbling block I need to remove from the path to my Father.

If he assaults me unjustly, then he just provided me with another opportunity to be like my Lord and please my Father.

The Lord orders my steps. At the end of the day, my enemy is the servant of the Lord to work what is pleasing in my Lord's sight. Since God is in charge of my life, I find great comfort in the fact that nothing can touch me that hasn't received His nod.

Behold, I Myself have created the smith who blows the fire of coals and brings out a weapon for its work; and I have created the destroyer to ruin. No weapon that is formed against you will prosper; and every tongue that accuses you in judgment you will condemn. This is the heritage of the servants of the Lord, and their vindication is from Me," declares the Lord. (Isaiah 54:16-17)

The Lord created the smith and the forge, the furnace and the hammer. It's as if He is saying to us: "I am the one who fans the fires that forge the weapons that will be used against you. So I will let you in on a little secret. I won't let the enemy create anything that will be able to destroy you!"

Think of it. The Lord created the one that forges the weapons used against you. And He gave you His armor to wear. He is on your side. He is cheering for you. Regardless of the weapons that come out of this forge, the Lord has made sure they won't have the power to destroy you. You will be victorious over every enemy. Every time.

༄

Benefit 8:
Strengthens Our Foundation

On October 17, 1989, a 6.9 magnitude earthquake shook Northern California. In the aftermath, sixty-three people died—forty-two from the collapse of the Nimitz Freeway—and over 3,700 were injured. About 12,000 homes and 2,600 businesses were damaged. Most could be repaired. Near the epicenter, forty buildings collapsed killing six people.

On January 12, 2010, there was a 7.0 magnitude earthquake in Haiti. Its devastating impact is not fully known, but the estimates are more than 160,000 (some estimates are as high as 316,000) deaths and 300,000 injured. According to the Haitian government, there were 250,000 residences and 30,000 businesses that had collapsed or suffered severe damage.

At the time of the earthquake in 1989, I was living about 60 miles northeast of the epicenter. At first I felt queasy, like I was going to pass out. Then I realized that my equilibrium was off because the ground was moving beneath my feet. I quickly grabbed my family and went to the center of the house, standing beneath a support beam between the kitchen and dining room. From that location, I looked through the picture window and saw my truck, which was parked in front of my house.

The trees and telephone poles were swaying back and forth like reeds in a strong wind. My truck was bouncing up and down like someone was using it as a springboard. The event lasted several minutes, and then everything went back to normal. Other than being shaken a bit, my family and I were no worse for wear.

Why was there so much more devastation in Haiti than in California? Scientific parameters give some explanation. There is a marked difference between a 6.9 and a 7.0 quake. Proximity and population density are also significant factors. But the primary reason, by far, has to do with the low-quality construction of Haiti's buildings. They collapsed because they weren't built to withstand the shaking. The death toll was high because people had been living and working in buildings that lacked the structural integrity to withstand the shock of the quake.

As a young man, I worked in construction shortly after I graduated from high school and continued well after graduating from Bible school. In fact, I continued in construction, working as a bi-vocational pastor for a number of years. During that time, I worked in California and experienced firsthand the building code requirements for both residential and commercial buildings. Any home or business built since the early 70s in California had to be constructed with enhanced methods to meet advanced building codes so it could withstand the force of an earthquake. Ordinances were passed that also required many buildings constructed prior to the implementation of these codes to be retrofitted to meet the current standards.

Without going into too much detail, let me just call attention to key aspects of these enhancements.

The first was in regard to the foundation. It had to be dug down to a certain depth and reinforced with a network of steel rods that were all tied together. The sheeting on the exterior and the sheetrock on the interior were completely covered with sheets that were staggered—nails were spaced every eight inches on the perimeter and twelve inches on the interior of the sheet. The joints and connections in the framing were reinforced with steel plates and connectors. Those are just a few of the additional requirements that were needed to increase the structural integrity.

It's interesting to note that the foundation is solid, but the building structures are made to be flexible. You can actually see buildings sway back and forth in an earthquake without being damaged.

Why does California require these extra construction components? Because they know that earthquakes will happen.

Why does God instruct us to be prepared to experience trials and tribulations?

And His voice shook the earth then, but now He has promised, saying, "Yet once more I will shake not only the earth, but also the heaven." This expression, "Yet once more," denotes the removing of those things which can be shaken, as of created things, so that those things which cannot be shaken may remain. Therefore, since we receive a kingdom which cannot be shaken, let us show gratitude, by which we may offer to God an acceptable service with reverence and awe; for our God is a consuming fire. (Hebrews 12:26-29)

This passage contains a promise—one assuring us that anything that can be shaken will be. Even though this is a sober revelation, we can lay hold of it with great encouragement.

Let me ask you this: Is there an area of your life that won't support God's purpose and destiny for you? Would you like Him to reveal that to you? If part of your foundation will collapse under the weight of your success and cause the loss of all you've built on it, would you like to fix it before it's too late? Since you're reading this book, I believe you would answer this the same way I have.

If there is an area of your life, ministry, marriage, family, career, etc. that is being shaken, then take heart. The Lord is helping you to see that there is an important part of your foundation needing repair or replacement. If you're being shaken, it's because you are standing on something other than the Kingdom of God, which can't be shaken. The shaking is for your benefit.

The shaking has started and it will continue, both personally and globally until there is nothing that hasn't been established in His kingdom. You can embrace this shaking as a gift because it will reveal the false hopes and securities in your faith and bring you into the reality of your unshakable identity in Jesus Christ.

As you not only endure but embrace the shaking, you'll be able to face the unknown future with utter confidence in the knowledge that you'll be prepared for whatever may come, whether for yourself or others.

CR80

* * *

Benefit 9:
Cultivates Compassion

There was a season in my life when I felt like the presence of the Holy Spirit lifted from my life. It happened just moments after I'd asked the Lord to be used in His kingdom with power.

A deep darkness engulfed my soul. I felt as if all light was stripped away from me. I cried out to the Lord, but heard no reply. A profound awareness of His absence arose, and fear gripped me by the throat. I felt the same hollow, empty feeling that I'd lived in before His Spirit filled my life. Dread, uncertainty. There was no peace, no joy, no love. It was a blackness that I can scarcely describe—as if I was in the middle of the ocean, in a storm, in the middle of the night. There was no light. No one to help. No hope of reaching shore. Only blackness and despair.

There was no emotion I could grab on to for assurance or comfort. There was only one thing I could hold on to—God's Word.

Regardless of what I was or wasn't feeling, God's Word was and is true. I told myself that it was impossible for God to leave me because He had promised through His Word, "I will never leave you nor forsake you." And He stated in Philippians 1:6 that "He who began a good work in you will perfect it until the day of Christ Jesus."

I wondered, *But had He begun a work in me?* Yes. The proof being that I wanted a relationship with Him, which was only possible if the Lord gave me that desire.

With these three truths, I endured several months constantly living with the sensation that I was lost and without God. In defiance of everything I was experiencing, I held on to His Word.

During that time, I'd sought counsel from other friends and pastors. No one could explain what was happening. We explored things that seemed obvious. Perhaps I had some sin that was hindering fellowship. Maybe it was a demonic attack. Regardless of what I did or what I thought, I couldn't hear from the Lord. I felt no comfort of His presence.

Then one day a friend of mine approached me and said he had a word for me. The word was *compassion*.

I thought it strange, but went to my Greek dictionary and looked it up. One of the words translated as *compassion* in the New Testament is *sumpathous*: **Sumpathoús (G4835), from sún (G4862), together or with, and páthos (G3806), suffering, misfortune.**

It literally means to be joined together with someone in his/her suffering. That revelation struck a chord within me. I sensed that it wasn't my own feelings I was feeling—I was experiencing something from someone else.

Within the next few days, I was ministering to a man a few years older than me, probably around 30 at the time. He told me that he was going through a divorce and struggling with the feeling that God had rejected him.

I said to him, "Let me see if I can describe what you're feeling. You feel a deep darkness has engulfed your soul, and you're crying out to the Lord but hearing no reply. You feel hollow and empty of love and peace, but are filled with fear and dread. You feel surrounded by a blackness that is like being in the middle of the ocean, in a storm, in the middle of the night with no light—with no one to help and no hope of reaching shore."

The man was amazed that I knew and could describe what he was going through so accurately. I told him that God had brought me through that same season so I would know how he was feeling and could share with him the promises of God for his life.

The man had thought that God had left him because of his divorce and was afraid that he had blasphemed the Holy Spirit, committing the unpardonable sin. I assured him that he hadn't and encouraged him through the Word and prayer. We both felt the Lord's presence that day.

There are times when the Lord will bring us through affliction so we are able to comfort others. Consider Paul's words in 2 Corinthians.

For just as the sufferings of Christ are ours in abundance, so also our comfort is abundant through Christ. But if we are afflicted, it is for your comfort and salvation; or if we are comforted, it is for your comfort, which is effective in the patient enduring of the same sufferings which we also suffer; and our hope for you is firmly grounded, knowing that as you are sharers of our sufferings, so also you are sharers of our comfort. (2 Corinthians 1:5-7)

By continuing further in that chapter, we see that what Paul and his team endure is no small trial. In fact, it's an affliction so severe that it pushes them beyond their own strength. In other words, they give up all hope of living.

For we do not want you to be unaware, brethren, of our affliction which came to us in Asia, that we were burdened excessively, beyond our strength, so that we despaired even of life; indeed, we had the sentence of death within ourselves so that we would not trust in ourselves, but in God who raises the dead; who delivered us from so great a peril of death, and will deliver us, He on whom we have set our hope. And He will yet deliver us, you also joining in helping us through your prayers, so that thanks may be given by many persons on our behalf for the favor bestowed on us through the prayers of many. (2 Corinthians 1:8-11)

Paul's and his companions' ability to bring comfort to the Corinthian church is purchased through a process Paul describes as excessive. In the book of Acts—as well as in his defense of his apostolic calling in 2 Corinthians 11:23-33—Paul endures a lot. From these types of circumstances, Paul can offer both compassion and comfort to those who are suffering affliction.

It's also important to note that in this passage, Paul describes another benefit extracted from their hardship—they have the sentence of death within them so they won't trust in themselves, but in God.

છ૪ૅ

* * *

Selah

Take a breath. Allow the thoughts and ideas we've covered in Section 1 to settle within your heart. This is the backdrop for the next leg of your journey.

You've learned to separate your individual story from the circumstances that are common to everyone. And you've learned to view your hardship as a tool in the hands of a loving God to reveal His nature and mold and shape His perfect plans and purposes in you. Fixing your eyes on the hope set before you prepared you to extract every treasure you can from the refining fires.

The challenges you've faced—as well as the ones you're facing now and the ones you'll face later—are for your benefit. They are working toward His great good for your life. With this perspective, you're ready to face your humanity. You're ready to visit the nature of humanity and discover how it interacts with injury, the world, and the spirit. These insights will further prepare you to focus on the challenges unique to you in Section 3.

CB&O

SECTION 2:

FACE YOUR HUMANITY

Chapter 6

Shifting Viewpoints

Today's focus determines tomorrow's reality. Religion tends to have a fixation on the behavior of sin instead of understanding the heart issues that fuel them. Challenging the cultural view of sin will help you look beyond the symptoms in your life to the wound in your soul.

You and I have covered quite a bit of ground so far to lay the foundation for this section. As we start to shift gears, I believe it's important to take a breath and prepare for what's next.

The subjects you're going to look at aren't easy to swallow. There are a lot of opinions on these topics from people trying to make sense of some things that just don't.

In this section, some things will be explained—and other things will make sense after you take the journey through to the other side. But I want to set the expectation that not everything will make sense. Not all questions will be answered. Neither do they have to be.

I'd like you to consider the possibility that what you've believed about your pain and hurts up to this point may not be accurate. If you and I knew everything we needed to know and had everything figured out, then we wouldn't need this book or ones like it.

I'm not suggesting all my viewpoints are correct or that yours are incorrect. I don't feel like an expert, and I certainly don't pretend to know all the answers. But I can testify that the Lord has helped me work through many of my sins and wounds, and I want to share with you the things He has used to help me.

The following thoughts, steps, tools, and processes are all part of what the Lord used to help my wife and me—as well as many others we've worked with—find freedom and healing.

I pray you will be at peace to sort through these things, using what works and dismissing the rest. If something here helps you to enter into a greater place in your relationship with the Lord or others—or yourself—it will be worth it.

The practical application of what you've been examining begins with directing your focus to the heart of your pain.

CR&O

Where We Focus

Any firefighter will tell you the way to fight fires has nothing to do with addressing the flames and everything to do with finding their source. The only effect pointing a fire hose toward the flames has is turning the water to steam. It might look spectacular, and the subsequent reaction is certainly impressive as the flames and water collide, but fires are not put out that way.

So often believers misdirect their focus—dealing with the effects of sin and not the source of it. The ravaging flames of sin concern us, as they should, and yet we must prepare to face the heat and look beyond the flames and smoke to find where they are coming from.

Whenever any of us tries to deal with sin by focusing on the result—instead of the source—those in sin and those trying to help them end up disappointed.

To have lasting freedom from sin, it must be cut off at the root. If we're to truly free ourselves or help free others, we'll need to take our eyes off of behavior and set them on the Lord, seeking His wisdom regarding the root of the behavior.

When believers try to address the sin instead of the root of the sin, the result is most often alienation—not restoration—of the ones struggling with sin. The alienated feel judged and unworthy, leading to rejection. The church feels frustrated and prone to blaming those individuals for not wanting to get serious with God.

A perfect example is divorce. I've heard it said that divorce is one of the greatest problems in the church today. I couldn't disagree more. Divorce is not the greatest problem. It's not even *a* problem in the church. **The real problem is that the church is full of hurting, immature believers who have a form of godliness, brought on by behavior modification, with no real power to walk out the life Christ has purchased for them.**

Statistically there are just as many marriages ending in divorce in the church as there are in the world. If there's no real difference between the success of a non-Christian marriage and that of a Christian marriage, I think it would be safe to say that we're truly missing something in how we've handled things up to this point.

So often it seems that the church does more to perpetuate brokenness in marriages that are going through divorce than it does to help it. Because divorce is looked upon as sin, well-meaning Christians feel compelled to decide who is to blame and take sides with the one who is so-called innocent.

Sermons are given on how divorce is a sin and shouldn't be an option. Well-meaning believers feel it incumbent upon themselves to point to the sin and compel the sinner to repent. As noble as it seems, that does nothing to heal the broken hearts of those who've become so desperate in their marriage that all they can think of doing is quit.

I submit to you that if we concern ourselves with mending broken hearts and discipling husbands and wives in the *how-tos* instead of the *should* and *should-nots*, we'll save more marriages. Avoiding divorce is not the goal. The goal is helping couples grow in healthy, loving, Christ-like marriages.

Believers who walk in victory over sin and bear lasting fruit for the Kingdom of God are those who've been healed and discipled at the heart level. Anyone can change behavior—at least for a few hours on Sunday and Wednesday. Some can even be religious all the time and practice white-knuckle Christianity, refusing to give in to sin out of sheer determination and self-righteousness.

Obviously that's not the Lord's plan for our existence on this earth. He hasn't called us to work harder at being good. He's called us to die and allow Him to live through us. He has called us to righteousness, peace, and joy. He has called us to abundant living. This life comes when we allow Him to point out our sin and the root beneath it. As we invite Him in to areas of our greatest need and surrender to His nature in us, we'll find we are free from the power of sin.

Jesus healed the sick, emotionally and spiritually, and then discipled them. That is the pattern we're called to follow. We need to see the greater need in people and bring healing and freedom to them, not be distracted by the ugliness of sin.

When the woman caught in adultery was brought before the Lord, He refused to look at her sin and refused to receive the accusations of others. To the contrary, He challenged her accusers with words that should echo in our hearts: "Let the one without sin cast the first stone." Her accusers dropped their rocks and went home. What happened? Jesus spoke life to the woman. He defended the one who was guilty from those who thought they were in a position to point to her sin. He didn't accuse her—He announced her forgiveness.

Straightening up, Jesus said to her, "Woman, where are they? Did no one condemn you?" She said, "No one, Lord." And Jesus said, "I do not condemn you, either. Go. From now on sin no more." (John 8:10-11)

We desperately need a paradigm shift in the church. We know we're to be a hospital for the world, but we've become a hospital that doesn't like sick or hurting people. Imagine how absurd it'd be if emergency room staff required people to shower, shave, and put clean clothes on before they could receive treatment! Or how unthinkable it would be if doctors scolded patients for having long-term illnesses or sustaining extensive injuries. Can you imagine being kicked out of the hospital because you didn't get well soon enough? How would you like to go to a hospital where they would welcome you as long as you kept your wounds sufficiently covered up?

If the church is truly a hospital, then it should be filled with the sick, wounded, broken, and bleeding. We should have a house full of sinners if we're doing our job—those who are well don't need a doctor! I suggest the real reason the world is avoiding the church is not because they don't know they need help—it's because they don't believe the church is really willing or even able to help them.

Another thing we must come to terms with is this: A physical hospital is gruesome and full of ugliness—so is a spiritual hospital. If you've ever made a trip to an emergency room, you can grasp the sometimes-brutal nature of medicine—blood, guts, and the like. Without reservation, I would say that I've been much more disturbed by the brutality of spiritual and emotional wounds than anything that could happen to a physical body.

It seems we're afraid that if we don't tell people how wrong their sin is that they will just continue to do it.

Oh, loved ones, we need to get our eyes off people's surface sins and open the hospital doors to all who are sick and wounded, weary and worn. That must start in our communities, churches, and in our homes. Where there is sin, God sees a wound. Sin is usually a substandard effort to meet a need or medicate a hurt.

Is an alcoholic just someone who needs to get sober? I'd say that God looks and sees a little child who was battered and abandoned and now, as an adult, feels ill-equipped to deal with life's problems. Some might look at a homosexual and see a perverted sinner. God looks and sees a child who was molested and now is desperately trying to make some sense of the swirling vortex of pain, feelings, and desires. What you and I call *sins* are, in most cases, nothing more than bandages and painkillers.

It may surprise you to know that most people don't want to sin, especially when it comes to Christians. They try not to sin, then feel guilty when they do. Ashamed and disappointed in themselves, they go to great lengths to hide and overcompensate for their lifestyles and choices. Why do they continue to do it? It's usually one or both of two reasons: They are sick/wounded or they just don't know how to deal with it.

In either case, our response should be the same. We're called to bring healing to the brokenhearted and make disciples of all nations.

In the Christian walk, there are two institutions: hospitals and schools. If you're hurting and wounded, then you need to get healed. Once that takes place, it's time to start school. All people are wounded to some degree, but it's reasonable to expect that some people can be treated as outpatients while they are attending school.

In both cases—hospital and school—the goal is for every person to be healed and graduate. Part of the problem in some churches is not that they don't allow the sinful and immature to come in, but that they aren't working to get them beyond it. As is so often the case when we become aware of a problem, we want to do what's right but swing to the other extreme. The place we must get to in the structure and function of the church is having an open door in and a plan to get people out into the world as healthy and fruitful members of the body of Christ.

Jesus loved and accepted everyone right where they were, but He made no secret about the fact He was calling them to something higher. So we too are called to live as He lived and walk as He walked. Those in the church, as well as those who come in, need to know two things: First, they are loved, accepted, and forgiven—and we as a body are committed to them. Secondly, our goal is to train and disciple them to become what God has called them to be.

In essence, we'd be communicating this: "It doesn't matter what you've done or what has been done to you, we love you, accept you, and are committed to helping you get healed, set free, and brought to maturity in the purposes that God has for your life."

We are neither condemning sin, nor condoning it. Sin isn't even the issue, righteousness is. Our call is not to condemn sin in the flesh, Jesus Christ already did that. Our call is to fix our eyes on Jesus, the author and finisher of our faith and to teach them to do the same.

This message is important for the body to understand on both the corporate and personal level. We need to begin examining the way we've done things as an organized body of believers and make the necessary adjustments so we can fulfill our God-given mandate to make disciples of every nation. These same principles apply to each of us as we work out our own salvation. It's only as individuals begin to walk in the revelation of God's plans and purposes that the greater organism begins to reflect that.

I certainly hope to challenge and encourage those who are called to lead and shepherd the flock of God in this hour. However, my main goal with this book is to provide you with practical tools that aid your process of healing and maturation. The problems I've mentioned regarding various mindsets in the church at large are often the very issues we struggle with on an individual level. These are the things that actually prevent us from finding the very freedom we are looking for and desperately need.

As we begin to walk through and apply the principles in this book to ourselves, it will release us to be a source of light and health in every area of our lives. Having the correct focus is critical, but with that focus, we also must have an understanding of what it is we are seeing.

CR&BO

Chapter 7

Empowered to Face
the Process

Along this journey, you'll need to assess your foundational beliefs. With a solid understanding of the gospel of the kingdom, you'll be empowered to face the challenges ahead.

The message of the gospel, according to the scriptures, is part of a story that takes time to understand. It's contained in a narrative stretching beyond the bounds of time into eternity. It's a love story, developed over centuries with heroes and villains, battles and victories, tragedies and celebrations. You're part of it and your role is still being discovered. It's vital to understand and fulfill your part in the culmination of this story—it's the story of Jesus Christ.

The first book I published—*Reclaiming Your Core: Restoring the Foundations of Faith*— was the last one I started to write. I'd spent over seventeen years teaching and using the messages in *Go Face Yourself*, but realized that without the foundation discussed in my first book, many people would struggle unnecessarily with the patterns of religious thought permeating the modern-day Western Church.

In all honesty and without any self-promoting motivations, I believe the book you're reading now can have an even greater impact if you get the foundational understanding outlined in my first book. Again, I'm not trying to increase book sales—as a matter of fact, if you can't afford my first book, please contact me and I'll send you a complimentary copy.

Even if you've been a believer your whole life and understand everything there is to know about the gospel message, you'll enjoy the review in that first book—a review the Lord brought my wife and me through in 2011, about five years prior to publishing it. I'd found there were a number of beliefs influencing me that were based on a religious spirit, traditions of men, and doctrines of demons. The outcome of that season was our returning to a simple view of the gospel message without its power getting diluted. The fruit shared in that short first book has been transformational in our lives and those who have read it.

Here are a few questions to help gauge your understanding of the foundations of the gospel message. Please answer yes or no after each question:

- Does your value as a believer increase when you do what is right?
- Does God get angry or disappointed with you when you sin?
- Has God punished you or will you be punished for your sins?
- Do you need to change your behavior in order for God to accept you?
- Are you free to live your life however you want since you are saved by grace?
- Has God done away with the Law?
- Does repentance mean you should stop bad behavior and start performing good behavior?
- Do you need to attend church, read your Bible, and pray in order to be okay with the Lord?

If you answered yes—or felt awkward, unsure, or uncomfortable when you answered no—to any of these questions, then there is a good possibility your understanding of the gospel may be under the influence of information that is not biblical. Please understand that I'm not suggesting these questions establish a criteria or are any indication of your relationship with the Lord. They are just a few questions that touch on some of the dynamics of our belief systems in a religious culture.

Even if you answered no to each question, can you explain from God's Word why that was the correct answer?

There are a few key truths you and I must establish in our hearts to effectively deal with the hurt, lies, and sins affecting our lives. As a believer, know this:

- The full price for your sin has been paid.
- You are called and commanded to confront your belief systems and bring yourself into agreement with the truth found in God's Word.
- You are called to live in and by the Spirit and to clothe yourself with Christ.
- You are called and commanded to die to your carnal and worldly nature.
- You have been completely forgiven—there's nothing you can do to pay for the things you've done wrong.
- You have been declared completely righteous—there's nothing you can do that will add to your righteousness.
- Neither your sin nor your good deeds have any impact on God's love for you.

Having a solid understanding of these truths—a foundation—helps to avoid expending useless effort on issues that have already been resolved. You are righteous. You have been forgiven. Since these have been accomplished for you, there's no need to spend one moment trying to gain them.

Instead, look objectively at the wounds, sins, and lies you believe about yourself, the Lord, and the world around you. That means having the proper perspective and seeing the working of your flesh and soul from the right angle. The only angle to access that information without being influenced by it is from the right hand of the Father. It's from the place of your spirit, where you're seated with Christ, that you must navigate the maze of your mind, will, and emotions. It's in that place that you are perfect and complete.

From that viewpoint, you're able to direct your soul through the quagmire of pain and misperception to the place of freedom. It's from that vantage point that you'll be able to identify the obstacles and make the necessary course corrections so you can enter into the fullness of life and joy purchased on the cross.

By viewing the details of this world and your life from His perspective—that is, from the place where you are seated in Him—you'll be empowered to face the process that lies before you.

CRBO

Courage Needed

Understanding information is one thing, but it won't provide what's needed to walk through what lies before you. Viewing your heart from a new perspective won't be enough. So while *understanding* the benefits is encouraging, you need to be armed with something more than knowledge. To press into these places, you need courage. This is it. This is what you've been preparing for—and it's not for the faint of heart.

You need courage to go through the process of facing pain. These areas in your heart are the places most often hidden behind your greatest fears. Fear is the door you must pass through. Fear of hurt. Fear of the unknown. Fear of rejection. Fear of failure. Fear of abandonment.

Fear stands as a sentinel for your wounds. The reason it guards and protects your wounds isn't to protect you from pain. **Fear wants to control you—and can only do that as long as it holds your wound hostage.** It wants you to think it's protecting you from further pain, but it just isn't true. It wants to spread your pain and perpetuate it in the lives of your loved ones. As long as fear can hold your pain, it can influence you, which is why it tries to intimidate you from facing it.

I've learned that fear is the great lie. It is a true enemy. It's the enemy you and I must face and defeat. We will need courage.

Courage comes from knowing that our Father loves us and has made a way for us to be free. The path to our freedom doesn't include running from our enemies. It leads straight into the lion's den. But in the lion's den, we'll discover our Father's power and the victory He has given us. His promise is this: We have an overwhelming abundance—more than we need—to conquer and rule over any enemy who stands before us.

Trust in the Lord with all your heart and do not lean on your own understanding. In all your ways acknowledge Him, and He will make your paths straight. (Proverbs 3:5-6)

Know that the Lord will guide you as you pursue Him through this process. The Holy Spirit will help you, heal you, and comfort you as you go, and you will be restored and made whole. That is His promise to you.

But now, thus says the Lord, your Creator, O Jacob, And He who formed you, O Israel, "Do not fear, for I have redeemed you; I have called you by name; you are Mine! When you pass through the waters, I will be with you; And through the rivers, they will not overflow you. When you walk through the fire, you will not be scorched, Nor will the flame burn you." (Isaiah 43:1-2)

The Lord will bring events and circumstances about that will be as fire that refines and water that cleanses. Remember that even as gold is refined, it is melted down in the fire. It is then that the **dross comes to the surface**—the ugliness of your wounds and the areas of your carnal nature that fostered the woundedness—brought out in these times to cleanse, heal, and make you victorious.

It takes courage and confidence in the work of the cross to face the ugliness that hides within the heart.

I'm not declaring that everyone will need to endure hardship or difficult circumstances to expose the heart's wounds. The reality is that we sometimes need extra assistance in getting to the hidden roots behind some of our beliefs and behaviors. In those times, don't be surprised if the heat is turned up in your life.

As mentioned before, the Lord is the one controlling the heat level of your enemy's forge. Will He allow the enemy to create anything that can actually harm you?

Absolutely not. Your Father loves you, He is for you and He says:

No weapon that is formed against you will prosper; And every tongue that accuses you in judgment you will condemn. This is the heritage of the servants of the Lord, And their vindication is from Me. (Isaiah 54:17)

And God who is faithful will not allow you to be tempted beyond what you are able. (I Corinthians 10:13b)

And we know that God causes all things to work together for good. (Romans 8:28a)

He will not fail you or forsake you. (Deuteronomy 31:8b)

He who began a good work in you will perfect it until the day of Christ Jesus. (Philippians 1:6b)

Be encouraged regardless of the circumstances you may face during this process. Recognize that the Lord is answering your prayer and exposing anything that might hinder you from walking in the fullness of life, love, and joy He has already purchased for you through Jesus Christ. Face this process with faith and confidence in the Lord—**God is on your side.** Know that His desire for you is to be conformed to the image of His Son. **He will work all things to that end.**

Armed with the courage to face the healing process, you're ready to examine how you were wounded in the first place.

CObCO

Chapter 8

Understanding the Wounding Process

What is an emotional wound? Examining and understanding the characteristics of a wound will better equip you for the healing process.

From the time we're born, the enemy begins his assault on our identity. Even before we know the Lord or understand good and evil, we have the fingerprint of the Father on our identity. The demonic realm and the world system hate us for it.

In 2013 the Lord brought me on a journey through my childhood—geographically and spiritually. He wanted me to revisit the places of my youth so He could speak to me about my identity. My wife and I traveled through various areas in Oregon and revisited places where a number of formative events took place. Many were fond memories, but amid the reminiscence were dark pockets of pain. With the counsel and support of my wife, I was able to visit each area of my heart that was exposed.

As I pondered events and circumstances of my youth, I discovered a recurrent theme. An abundance of lies infused my pain. Lies I believed about myself, my loved ones, and the Lord. Their singular purpose was to destroy my identity when I was a young man.

The result—of circumstances mixed with those lies—was a number of conclusions I'd made with the help of the enemy. Those conclusions undermined my understanding of who I really was and am. So I took measures. Measures of self-protection and self-preservation, based on the flesh and rooted in pain and confusion. The result was living my life with an identity imposed on me, which led me away from the identity my Father in heaven had given me.

The enemy of our soul has one fear—we'll come to know who we really are. Helping you recapture the reality of who you are is at the heart of this book.

You are an amazing creation formed with love and intention to be exactly the way you are. Unique in all of creation, there is no one quite like you. You were fashioned with certain gifts, talents, abilities, personality, likes, and dislikes to be a perfect expression of the One who created you. You were designed to connect with your brothers and sisters in Christ to bring your vitally important expression to His body. You were birthed out of eternity from which your Heavenly Father dreamed about you and how you, His precious child, would look, act, and feel. It brought Him such joy to bring you out of the hidden place of His heart to present you to the rest of His creation.

He also knew every event of your life before you even took your first breath. He knows your pain and knows your trials. In your distress, He is distressed. Because He knew these things would come upon you, He also gave you everything you needed before you needed it. He placed within you the ability to overcome. You can be 100% sure that everything you have gone through or ever will face will be used to further His wonderful purpose in you. The plans He has for you have taken into account every desire and passion He has planted in your heart. No matter how challenging the process will be, once you are through it, you'll be glad you chose His path.

As you navigate the complexities of thoughts, beliefs, and emotions that surround the wounds in your soul, be mindful of the impact on your identity. You can trust that the process you are going through is designed to bring you clarity regarding your true identity in Christ. In reality it doesn't matter where you start the process because the destination is the same. It's just like climbing a mountain. It doesn't matter which valley you're in. Your path will lead one way—up.

Understanding that the nature of the wound has to do with the assault on your identity will help keep you moving in the right direction. It's also important to take a deeper, more granular look at how the wounding process works so you can dismantle the work of the enemy that surrounds it. For that, you'll need to understand the anatomy of the wound.

CR80

Anatomy of a Wound

A wound is defined as an injury to living tissue caused by a cut, blow, or other impact, typically one in which the skin is cut or broken. To examine the impact on your soul, let's consider a wound to be anything having a negative impact on your identity, belief systems, or sense of well-being.

Charlie is a thinker. As a boy, he spent a lot of time daydreaming and coming up with creative ideas to impact the world around him. For him, spending an afternoon finding the objects and animals in the clouds as they floated by was time well spent.

Charlie's dad was a doer. He couldn't understand why it was so hard for Charlie to just do his chores and show some effort around the farm. He often scolded Charlie and had various terms to describe his son that etched away at his identity. Instead of celebrating his creativity, he saw him as lazy and lacking motivation.

One afternoon the neighbor came to visit with his wife and their twelve-year-old daughter. Suzy, who was Charlie's age and in the same classes at school, had just received an award for her performance at a piano recital.

The parents were proud of their daughter and talked about how bright and talented she was. Charlie's dad was impressed.

Charlie felt a little awkward because he really liked Suzy and wanted her to know it, without being too obvious. He sat in the room, quietly enjoying the company of Suzy while the parents chatted.

Charlie's dad congratulated Suzy and her parents on her accomplishments. Then he said, "I wish Charlie would learn to do something worthwhile. The kid is lazy and doesn't do anything around here. I don't think he's even smart enough to do something like Suzy."

His dad's words had bruised him before, but these words pierced his heart and shattered any sense of worth he'd mustered up to that point. He was humiliated in front of his friend and her parents. But worse than that, he saw an image of himself from his own father, convincing him that he was worthless and couldn't do anything right.

From that day on, Charlie did everything he could to try to get his dad to see some value in him. Something of worth. But nothing was ever good enough to warrant a compliment or a word of affirmation. No matter how thorough he tried to be, there was always something that could have been done better. Something missing. Something undone.

Charlie tried until he was out of high school, and then decided he wanted to pursue a career in journalism. His dad said, "Of course you would pick something that wouldn't require you to actually work! That's what any lazy person would choose. Why can't you just do something worthwhile with your life?"

Not only was Charlie's dream shattered, but so was his hope of ever being good enough for his dad. Instead of trying to prove he was worth something, he decided his dad must be right. So he committed himself to being the worthless deviant his father told him he was. He spent the majority of his 20s pursuing a lifestyle of drugs, alcohol, and promiscuous relationships. Anything he felt a worthless person would do—that's what he did.

Let's examine the individual components of Charlie's wound.

The Initial Wound

Wounds can occur in any number of ways, but usually at the heart of a wound is at least one of these:

- An unmet need (real or felt)
- A violation of trust
- Inappropriate or misunderstood behavior

In Charlie's case all three took place. He had a need for a safe environment where he could cultivate his identity. His father not only failed to provide for that need, he also violated his son's trust and behaved inappropriately toward him.

At the heart of the wounding process is the distortion of our true identity.

The Offense

As a result, this wound created an offense in Charlie's soul. A wound turns into an offense when it is interpreted by our own perceptions. We judge the actions—or lack of action—to be wrong within ourselves. This offense creates the perception of a debt owed to us, an injustice. Without forgiveness, the offense remains lodged within the soul indefinitely.

In that moment, Charlie judged his father and determined that his father didn't love him and had rejected him.

The Reaction

Tied to every offense is a reaction. That reaction is closely tied with the lies we believe about the events and circumstances surrounding our wound. The enemy of our soul is quick to whisper into the ear of a wounded person—especially a child—to *help* them interpret these events.

The reaction Charlie felt was rejection and shame. This intense pain required a response; it required an explanation. It needed to be interpreted and understood in the mind of this twelve-year-old boy.

The Response

When we experience an offense, we're compelled to come up with a conclusion about the wound. In this case, Charlie's conclusion was that he must be the problem—there must be something wrong with him. Not even his father could accept or approve of him. In Charlie's mind, he wasn't worthy of his father's love because he had failed at meeting his father's expectations. Charlie believed he was flawed, deserving to be ridiculed and mistreated.

The traumatic events in our lives—emotional, spiritual, or circumstantial—have the power to change our view of ourselves. It's our identity that is beaten, battered, and torn. And it is from our identity, our perception of our self, that we live our lives.

The Result

Unhealed wounds/unresolved issues cause fissures in the very fabric and foundation of our lives. They undermine our ability to build solid, healthy relational structures in our lives.

If not properly treated, a wound will become infected. This infection increases the damage, widens the impact area, and can spread throughout the body. If neglected, a simple, untreated wound can result in death.

This wounding process culminates in the development of our belief systems. These are the systems that drive every decision we make. Regardless of my capacity, if I don't believe I'm capable of doing something, I will never try. Conversely, if I believe that I'm something, my thought processes will bring me in to the circumstantial dynamics that, in my mind, will confirm that my beliefs are correct. Even if those circumstances are deplorable, there will be a part of my belief system that convinces me that it's normal.

Barriers and Bandages

In an attempt to protect our wounds, we create amazingly intricate mechanisms to place barriers between our hurts and those we fear may hurt us more. Most of this takes place on a subconscious level—and seems quite normal.

We can create masterful internal stories to explain and justify our thoughts, feelings, beliefs, and behaviors. These are manifested through our internal dialog and self-talk.

One of the greatest struggles I've had throughout my life has been a fear of rejection. This fear was rooted in a series of wounds that took place at various stages of my development and permeated every area of my life. Because I saw every relationship as a potential threat, I'd erected barriers around myself in hopes of minimizing the chances of getting close to someone who'd end up rejecting me.

When I felt myself starting to get close to someone, I'd say or do things that would give them a reason to reject me. In my internal dialog, I'd say, *If they really love me, they will still accept me.* In effect I would push people away from me in hopes that they wouldn't leave, but would *love me enough* to push beyond the reasons to reject me. The comfort I had was that if they didn't stay in relationship with me, then I had rejected them before they had a chance to reject me.

It seemed to make sense to me at the time, but as the Lord began to heal the wound in my identity, I realized these were all fear-based methods designed to protect myself instead of trusting the Lord. I also recognized the irony that the very mechanism I had created to protect myself, drove away many people who did care about me and wanted to be in relationship with me. My barriers not only failed to protect me, they actually deepened my pain.

At one point in the healing process, the Lord showed me that it was like wrapping myself in barbed wire and forcing anyone who said they loved me to prove it by embracing the pain of being near me. Not only did I place a confusing and unfair barrier around my life, I judged people for their unwillingness to embrace a pain that I wasn't even willing to accept myself.

You may be able to identify with this example. Either way, the chances are quite high that you have barriers around the hurts of your heart that not only aren't helping, but are probably hurting you and those around you.

Such is the nature of our attempts to protect ourselves. Our wound will not be healed while it's covered with barriers and bandages. Short-term solutions only cover the pain. As we work through the process of exposing and identifying our wounds, we will also discover how we have tried to protect and cover them.

Medication

Sometimes it feels like the pain in our life is unbearable. It's in those times that there's a strong temptation to look for something that will medicate us. I say *temptation* because most often the things we look to for comfort lead us away from the fullness of life promised by the Lord.

Drugs, alcohol, pornography, and things like these hold a promise of relief but don't truly deliver. There are much more socially acceptable forms of medication that are just as dangerous: overeating, religion, and codependent relationships, to name a few. Anything we use to diminish the pain of our past is a form of medication. Although it may seem necessary, it actually can hinder our healing process by preventing us from having a full understanding of the wounds we carry.

I know it may be challenging to accept, but there is no medication prescribed by the Lord to help us cope with our pain. His solution is to provide His power so we can walk *through* the pain to complete healing and restoration. There's no anesthesia during the process because He wants us to be present with a clear mind as we take each step in our journey to wholeness.

Know this: Your hope can rest securely in the knowledge that He has given you His grace—that is to say, He already has given you everything you need for this process. Regardless of what you may feel in the moment, it can't change the truth of His Eternal Word.

Understanding the anatomy of your wounds and the dynamics of your life connected to them will help uncover the areas in your soul affecting your identity.

As you and I move forward, I'll discuss some indicators to help identify where you may have unhealed wounds. But first, you're going to need some tools.

CR80

Chapter 9

Filling Your Toolbox

The flesh and the soul interact with the wounds of the heart. What does it look like when the carnal nature is taking the lead? Here is where you discover tools that help you find the troubled areas.

Getting to the root of your wounds is going to take some detective work—learning how to look for and recognize the clues.

In Galatians 5, there are two sets of identifying traits: one of the flesh; the other of the Spirit. Since our wounds are rooted in the flesh and connected to the soul, recognizing the source of certain behaviors can provide a lot of insight into which areas we're not experiencing the fullness God has for us.

The converse is also true. Areas that aren't bearing the fruit of the Spirit can be an indication that something needs to be addressed. First, let's examine some clues regarding the works of the flesh.

Now the deeds of the flesh are evident, which are: immorality, impurity, sensuality, idolatry, sorcery, enmities, strife, jealousy, outbursts of anger, disputes, dissensions, factions, envying, drunkenness, carousing, and things like these, of which I forewarn you, just as I have forewarned you, that those who practice such things will not inherit the kingdom of God. (Galatians 5:19-21)

This passage isn't a list of dos and don'ts. It is a tool to help identify when your flesh is creating a problem. Think of it as lights on a car's dashboard. If you see a red light that looks like an oilcan, you know the oil is low. Likewise, if you're regularly exhibiting behaviors consistent with the works of the flesh, that's your warning light that some issues need to be addressed.

It is vitally important to use this tool the way it's intended—to identify the areas that need healing and restoration. Religion tries to convince us that we need to address the works of the flesh by changing our behavior. That's the equivalent of putting a piece of tape over the light on our dashboard. We may be able to mask the warning sign, but that does nothing to address the need that the behavior represents.

We must approach this process from the understanding that God gave us our righteousness and value—apart from our input or effort. If the works of the flesh are being manifested, it isn't a call to feel guilty and ashamed. It's simply the Lord inviting us to be healed and set free. Just like the light on the dashboard. That light wasn't placed there to rebuke us or to tell us we're horrible drivers. It's there to let us know something needs attention. It's there to keep our vehicle from breaking down and to keep it running at peak efficiency.

So know this: God has wired you like that dashboard light. He is for you and wants to help you identify the things in your life that are preventing you from experiencing the fullness of life, love, and joy that He has already provided for you.

Now let's examine some important dynamics within this passage that reveal how the flesh operates. There are two different aspects of the works of the flesh—behaviors and emotional responses. Let's start with behaviors.

CRBO

Sensuality

Sexual behavior that functions outside of a healthy expression in marriage is rooted in the flesh. This is a very complex subject—volumes have been written about it—so we won't delve into those depths here. However, examining components of the flesh's sensual works may reveal the existence of a wound.

Gary was a young, attractive man in his late 20s. As a believer, he struggled a lot with the guilt and shame of not only his current battle with pornography, but also his history of promiscuity. By the time Gary reached adulthood, he'd already had over one hundred sexual partners. And even though he was now married, he couldn't seem to break free from the temptation to look for and desire sexual encounters.

As he journeyed beneath the works of the flesh, he was able to trace his behavior to the root.

When Gary was in grade school, he was lured into a trusted neighbor's house. A pedophile. The neighbor gave him ice cream and asked if he wanted to watch a movie—pornography. While the images were displaying on the TV, Gary was molested.

The pain, shame, and confusion of this event caused a deep crisis in Gary's identity. He began running from the pain—as well as pursuing a sense of his masculine identity—by having sex with any girl who would allow it. Far from validating his identity, his sexual behavior created an addiction the enemy used to continually tear away the sense of who Gary really was in the Lord.

Sensual behavior connected to a wound will never be able to bring a true sense of value or restoration to your identity. Most often it just becomes something used to either cover or medicate pain. Here are some questions to help identify if your actions are rooted in a wound.

Am I using my sexuality . . .

- as a way to escape painful feelings?
- as a way to validate my sense of worth?
- to comfort myself?
- to find relief from stress or anxiousness?

- to feel a sense of belonging or a connection with someone?

Does my sexual activity . . .
- make me feel uncomfortable?
- cause feelings of shame?
- make me feel powerful or validated?

Sexual activity can be a powerful tool in the hands of the enemy to bring destruction to you and your relationships. It also can be a powerful tool to cultivate intimacy and closeness with your spouse when submitted to the Holy Spirit.

The enemy targets sexuality because of the power it has to touch the deepest parts of the soul. God created sexual intimacy as a tool so man and woman could become one flesh. It's a level of unity and intimacy not possible in any other way. Many wounded people use sexual activity to feel loved and accepted by another person. This feeling of closeness and intimacy can only temporarily pacify the need of the heart to be loved and accepted.

The framework of these kinds of relationships are supported only by the flesh and are unable to bring a person into a place of wholeness. They can never provide the true and deep needs of the heart. Quite the contrary is true—they are roadblocks to healing.

The physiological effects on the brain enhance the power of sexual activity. Sexual activity is a physical act that works with the brain to produce encounters that feel amazing. During a sensual encounter, the chemicals released heighten awareness and increase the sense of well-being and satisfaction. That's why sexual activity, even without a partner, can be so desirable as a way to ease our pain or help us feel good about ourselves. It's also why it can become an addiction.

Promiscuity, pornography, and other forms of inappropriate sexual behavior are great at accomplishing two things—providing temporary pleasure and increasing pain. As it is with most addictive cycles, the temporary pleasure digs the hole in our heart just a little bit deeper. The next time we try to fill the hole, we feel the need to add something more.

If this is one of the works of the flesh you find manifesting in your life, don't be discouraged. As you get to the root of the pain, discover the wounds and find healing, you won't need to look in other places for what you need. There are a lot of resources available to help with the complexities of this addiction. Dealing with the wounds in your heart will go a long way toward empowering you in this journey.

Know that your Father in Heaven loves you and is able to heal and restore your sexuality. You can't sin so badly that He can't forgive and heal you.

ೞೲ

Idolatry

Idolatry is another subject that we often dismiss because we really don't bow down and pray to statues and carvings of deities. Some believers have relegated the topic to the modern equivalency of trusting money, which is certainly a form of idolatry. Sadly, idolatry is quite common in the world today and unknowingly practiced by most people in one form or another.

Simply defined, idolatry is the act of looking to someone or something other than the Lord for what He promises to provide.

As I shared previously, after my divorce in 2000, I was desperate to find someone to marry. I didn't want to face my life alone. I didn't want to be a single father. I didn't want to be a celibate.

The woman I pursued gave me an opportunity to have what I wanted and what I was seeking. The problem was, I was trying to find in her something that's only found in the Lord. I wanted her to make me feel valued, wanted, respected. I wanted her to make me feel secure and connected, removing my loneliness and fear. I was looking to her for things God had promised to provide. I had made her into an idol.

After my second divorce, I resolved that I wasn't going to pursue any other relationships until the Lord led me. I'd recognized that there were some predictable patterns taking place in my life pertaining to relationships. As I surveyed the landscape of my life, I could point to similar circumstances with a number of people who weren't connected. It dawned on me that all these people had only one thing in common—me.

Even though I didn't know what it was, I knew there was something in me that needed to change. For the first time in my life—since my sexuality was stirred as a teenager—I surrendered it to the Lord. I surrendered my desire for a wife and female companionship. I surrendered the last of what my flesh was holding on to and once again gave the Lord permission to do whatever was needed to make me the man He created me to be.

The Lord brought me through a process of identifying, and subsequently destroying, many idols in my life. Jobs, finances, relationships, approval, and other things that had become my idols. I'd looked to each one of these things to varying degrees to provide something for me. In each case, what I sought proved unreliable. There was only one dependable source. God is my comfort, my joy, my security, and my source of approval and validation.

Take some time to consider if there are relationships or circumstances you feel need to be a certain way to feel good, secure, valued, etc. These are great indicators that the Lord is ready to bring healing to those areas.

☙❧

Sorcery

Most of the images that come to mind when we think of sorcery or witchcraft have to do with dark-natured individuals involved in demonic rituals and incantations. Although there are some who participate in such activities, sorcery isn't limited to those extremes.

5331. pharmakeia; gen. pharmakeias, fem. noun from phármakon (n.f.), a drug, a word Greek writers used for curative as well as medicinal or poisonous drugs. Pharmakeia means the occult, sorcery, witchcraft, illicit pharmaceuticals, trance, magical incantation with drugs

The root of the word *sorcery* in the Greek is the same for another word—*pharmacy*. One aspect of sorcery is the use of drugs, legal or illegal, for the purpose of creating a state of mind that intentionally alters our life experience. Using drugs and alcohol to have fun, forget our troubles, or medicate our emotional pain is a mechanism to avoid addressing issues of our lives in a healthy and productive manner.

Let me be clear that I'm not saying medications are bad, nor am I suggesting there is no place for pharmaceutical intervention. Let me also clearly state for the record that I'm not making a statement regarding the use of alcohol—whether or not we should imbibe.

The issue being examined here is specifically about how it relates to inner healing. Whether drinking alcohol is right or wrong is not the issue. The use of drugs or alcohol as a work of the flesh relates specifically to the purpose of its use—are drugs or alcohol being used to mask or medicate an area that the Lord wants to heal?

Using chemicals to cope with the emotional difficulties in life is a work of the flesh that will do nothing to help you or me enter into the fullness of life available to us in Christ. So if this is an area of struggle, then it could be another clue that it's something for you to pray about. There may be something beneath the behavior that needs the healing touch of our Father.

As with sexual and other forms of addiction, there are many resources available to help you walk through the process of recovery. The best course of action I recommend is to begin with a process that addresses the core issues of identity and brings healing to the wounds of the past that precipitated the addictive behavior. I've seen numerous people delivered from addictive lifestyles by reclaiming the core of their true identity in Christ and applying the methods discussed in this book.

At the very least, knowing who you are in Christ and finding healing and restoration in your soul will become a powerful foundation for you as you journey through the addiction-recovery process.

∽∙∾

Witchcraft

The use of witchcraft often involves the act or process of using potions, spells, incantations, and/or other external forces to bring about a predetermined outcome. At the core, it relates to issues of power, control, and manipulation. I believe witchcraft—as a work of the flesh—is the process of trying to manipulate people to be for us what we want them to be.

This definition may or may not be correct, but I have repeatedly observed this behavior at work within the relational dynamics of wounded people. Myself included.

One of the negative impacts of the dysfunctional environment of my youth was that it created within me a fear of the unknown.

Helen and I had only been married a few months when she started acting differently whenever we were around other people. I noticed she was calling a number of people, but not talking loudly enough for me to hear. At church I could see she'd been talking with a few people when I wasn't nearby, but had stopped talking when I got within earshot. I knew something was going on, but didn't know what it was.

There were only a few clues, a few minor slips. But it was enough for me to confront her. I knew something was going on and I wasn't included in it. I approached Helen with a raised voice and a red face. I demanded she tell me what was going on and what it was she was trying to hide. At first she tried to play it off, but I wouldn't have it. Finally, she gave in and told me: She wanted my birthday to be special and had been planning a surprise birthday party for me with my friends and family.

By that time, I'd made such an issue of it that we ended up canceling the party. I didn't know it at the time, but what I was doing was attempting to manipulate and control her to prevent her from hiding anything from me. Because of my fear of the unknown or unpredictable, I used intimidating behavior to produce the outcome that I wanted.

These types of attempts at control and manipulation are common among wounded people. Because of the unpredictable—and in some cases, violent—environments people grow up in, they are insecure in situations where they don't feel in control. This leads to a powerful compulsion to be able to predict outcomes. Even if the outcome is destructive to themselves or others.

For years I was puzzled at the rate with which people who were rescued from violent relationships returned to the situations they were rescued from. However, the pieces of the puzzle came together as the Lord showed me how I was doing the same things, just in a different way.

If you find yourself with the compulsion to control or manipulate people in your life, it may be a good indication an area of your life is depending on the flesh.

CR80

Chapter 10

Flesh-Empowered Emotions

Your emotions—just like your behaviors—can help you identify areas of your heart that may need healing.

We are wired for emotions. Emotions, in and of themselves, are neither good nor bad, neither right nor wrong. They're part of the human design, given as tools to express our hearts, thoughts, ideas, and feelings.

As we examine the emotional works of the flesh, we'll see there are times when our emotional reaction is rooted in something contrary to our well-being or the benefit of others. That reaction is a reflection of something amiss in our soul. By design, it brings to the surface things hidden in our hearts.

When we examine our emotional responses honestly, we'll see a need to discover what's lying at the heart of that emotion. Just like smoke indicates a fire, so too our flesh-empowered emotions give us clues of where we need to look for the embers of our own pain.

൚

Destructive Anger

Often times, when our identity has been wounded, our emotions become the vehicle we use to express the pain we're feeling. In these situations, powerful emotional responses of anger can help us track down areas in our hearts that are being assaulted by past events.

Even though I understand that anger is one of our basic emotions, I seldom identify anger as a primary emotion. Most often it's the evidence of other masked emotions. As a work of the flesh, our natural, basic emotion of anger goes beyond healthy expression and becomes outbursts of rage, arguments, disputes—and the cause of strife and division.

Anger is an emotion that is the response to perceived provocation, hurt, or threat. When we're consistently experiencing anger, it's often an indication something deeper is going on. Our ability to look beneath the anger to see the source is a powerful tool in our pursuit of healing. Asking a few simple questions can go a long way toward understanding why we respond the way we do in certain situations.

- What's at the source of my anger?
- Is this situation causing me to feel hurt?
- Is it touching on something that I fear?
- Does this situation remind me of a past event that caused me pain or fear?

When I was about ten years old, an older boy approached me, asking if I wanted to be a man. Of course, at that age, those thoughts were important to me, so I told him that I did. He invited me to his house under the pretense of helping me become a man—when, in fact, what happened made that process very difficult. He molested me and said that was my proof that I wasn't gay.

Not fully understanding what had happened, I shared this with an adult and several other kids who were older than me. The boys I shared it with were disgusted, and the adult completely ignored me. I felt embarrassed, ashamed, and violated.

The feelings of hurt and confusion turned to bitterness, hatred, and anger. From that time on, if anyone called me gay or questioned my perceived manhood, I would explode. More than a few guys were punched in the face as a result of my anger. Not only would I lash out in anger if my masculinity was challenged, I also developed a hatred for those who I thought were gay, whether they actually were or not.

There was one young man who I bullied regularly because he had the unfortunate experience of having an erection in the boy's locker room. Unexplained and inconveniently timed erections are a natural part of puberty and had nothing to do with this boy's sexuality. But for me, it was a reminder of my own wound—and I hated him for it.

As a side note, when the Lord had healed my wound, I thought a lot about the pain I had unfairly caused that young man. I had confessed my sin before the Father and asked the Lord to heal and bless that man and redeem him from the pain I had caused. I was actually able to find him to apologize and ask him for forgiveness. He was very gracious and kind with me, and we've stayed in contact since then.

That event and the subsequent process of healing and restoration the Lord brought me through could be an entire book in and of itself.

For me, it wasn't that I was some angry, mean-spirited kid who was opposed to a certain sexual lifestyle. The primary issue was that I was wounded and my identity was under assault. The pain surrounding my struggle to know who I was resulted in a violent manifestation of anger. I'm not saying that to justify or excuse my abusive behavior. I only state it as a fact that helped me understand there was a real issue beneath the sin. Many times I had struggled with attempts to control my behavior, but in the moment those memories were triggered, the intensity of the pain was beyond my ability to control.

Without going too deep, there are a few things I'd like to share regarding my process of healing. When the Lord showed me the source of my anger and hatred regarding sexuality, I came to understand the struggle wasn't about what was right or wrong for someone else to do. It was the crisis of my own struggle with understanding myself and knowing who I was. Because this subject represented a fracture in my own identity, it became an external focal point to direct my pain.

My external behavior was an indication of the level of pain I felt internally. When the Lord healed the wound and restored my identity in Him, my beliefs and behaviors were transformed.

Recognizing and understanding our anger and how the flesh will use it can help us get to the heart of painful issues. If anger has been or is a struggle for you, it may be a great indication that there is a belief system beneath the surface that is cooperating with your flesh for self-protection.

❧

Jealousy

When the Lord began speaking to me about the issue of jealousy, I was confused. Up to that time, I'd thought jealousy meant wanting material things other people had. That didn't apply to me.

I learned there was much more to this emotion than I'd realized. In the context of Galatians 5:20, it refers to a self-centered zeal that resents the good someone else enjoys. I further discovered it also refers to being "fearful or wary of being supplanted; apprehensive of losing affection or position" and "intolerant of disloyalty or infidelity." Contrasting attitudes would be confident, tolerant, trusting, understanding and generous.

That's when it began to make sense. These were definitely areas I'd struggled with in my relationships. A deep pain stirred in me when I felt a person I loved—or desired affection and attention from—ignored my perceived needs and desires or showed attention and affection to others. My zeal was to have their affirmation and attention directed toward me.

That revelation helped me see how jealousy was manifesting in my life through the flesh. The Lord used it to help me discover a belief system connected with several deep wounds. At the core of this work of the flesh were deep-rooted fears of rejection and abandonment. He initiated a process of healing—without which it would've been impossible to have healthy relationships.

I realized that this area of woundedness not only contributed to my relational challenges, but in many ways it was causing them. The work of jealousy was the smoke that led me to the fire.

Having an understanding of the flesh and how it works is a powerful arsenal in your healing journey. The toolset I prefer—and find even more valuable—is having clarity about the fruit of the Holy Spirit.

ⳍ

The Fruit of the Spirit

Once again, this isn't a list of dos. Fruit is the byproduct of the type of tree that bears it. When we're walking in agreement with the Holy Spirit, there will be evidence produced in our lives. This evidence isn't produced by our efforts—if it was by our efforts, it would be works. The natural byproduct when an area of your life is walking in agreement with the Spirit is this: It's marked by one or more of His fruits.

But the fruit of the Spirit is love, joy, peace, patience, kindness, goodness, faithfulness, gentleness, self-control; against such things there is no law. (Galatians 5:22-23)

If we are in the midst of circumstantial dynamics not marked by the fruit of the Spirit, then it may very well be an indication something needs our attention.

When walking in agreement with the flesh, we see works of the flesh in our efforts. When walking in agreement with the Spirit, we see His fruit. If we're not experiencing His fruit, then we are agreeing with something that isn't true.

Periodically Helen and I happen upon a subject of disagreement. Sometimes I am completely and utterly confident that I am correct—and she is, well, not. During the course of our dialogue, there may even be times when I become agitated and argumentative. In those moments, it's easy for me to blame her for my agitation since she's obviously wrong, but I'm still unwilling to yield her position. My agitation can move into anger and frustration—depending on the sensitivity of the subject—and my being disrespectful presenting my case, forceful in my passion about the subject.

Here's my point. Objectively, I was correct. From a spiritual and emotional standpoint, I was completely in the flesh. In retrospect, I can see there was a certain moment when I shifted from abiding in the Spirit to working in my flesh.

When you and I consistently experience situations where we lose peace, patience, kindness, etc., we have a clue there may be some belief systems or wounds ready to be addressed.

Now that you have a backdrop of how the works of the flesh and fruit of the Spirit can provide tools to expose problem areas, it's time to learn to identify the actual wound.

CRBO

Chapter 11

Identifying Old Wounds

Traumatic experiences can have a perpetually negative impact on your life and relationships. Learning how they interact with your behaviors, emotions, and relationships will give you clues of where they're hiding. Here you'll find some general guidelines to keep in mind as you step closer to the specific wounds that are unique to you.

Imagine you had a festering wound on your leg covered beneath your pants. By all external appearances, you're fine, but wait until someone pokes you or bumps into your leg. Immediately and with great intensity, pain shoots through your body. The agony temporarily incapacitates you. It wouldn't be too hard to imagine that you might react strongly, possibly with violence, to get the person away from your wound.

From a spiritual and emotional standpoint, that is exactly what's happening in us and in those around us. Unlike a physical wound, it's much easier to miss the fact that we may be the problem and not necessarily those around us.

So often when we experience pain in a relationship, we start to avoid the relationship. We see the other person as the problem instead of considering there may be some issues we need to work through ourselves. Pain in relationships is a perfect indicator that there are areas of our own heart that may need healing.

● ● ●

Of course, not all pain is a result of our own need for healing, because there are legitimate emotional reactions from others who hurt us. However, many times the depth of pain we feel is disproportionate to the actual offense committed against us. Just as a person poking a healthy leg may cause an irritation—or possibly even a painful response—it's nothing compared to being poked in the middle of an open wound.

Most people seem to end up suffering the same types of hurts over and over again. We may come up with cliché statements to minimize and explain hurts away, but what if there was a reason for it? If we truly believe we serve a God who is madly in love with us and is passionately concerned about our abundant life, then it shouldn't be too much of a stretch to imagine that He may be orchestrating circumstances to help us get there. I'm convinced the Lord will actually bring people into our lives who will help expose those wounds so we can be healed.

When we feel the sting of emotional pain in relationships, it's a good time to step back and ask the Lord why we feel the way we do. When we stop running from the pain and start bringing it to the Lord, we will find true healing and permanent freedom from that pain.

There is a call to faith in this process. We have to believe and hold to the truth that God is working in our lives and causing all things to work together for good. If we hold on to this, we will be able to lean on the strength the Lord supplies to bring us through the wound-healing process.

In the past when others touched a wound, it hurt. That hurt will happen again when the Lord touches it. The point is, the wound will hurt either way—regardless if the intent is healing (from the Lord) or harm (from someone else).

The reason I say that is because we've developed a natural barrier of protection around the hurts of our past. We have made vows like *I will never let anyone hurt me like that again* and *I will never trust anyone again* to try and keep potential victimizers at a distance. To a certain extent it works, even though sooner or later we let someone close enough to hurt us and remind us of how we need to protect ourselves even more.

When we come to the Lord and invite Him into the pain of our past, we have to let those walls down. The Lord comes in, past all our protective barriers and patterned responses, and touches the heart of our pain. He goes all the way back to the place where it started. The pain and emotions we originally felt often come rushing past our layers of denial and into our conscious mind—and we experience the original offense all over again.

"Why would I want to do that?" you might ask. Because when the Lord visits your wound, it's for the purpose of healing. Even though it will hurt, the knowledge that you won't have to live under the wound's crippling effects anymore will give you hope. Another reason is that you know you can trust the Lord. He is honest in his discipline and healing—*faithful are the wounds of a friend,* as Proverbs 27:6 teaches. The Lord is tender and compassionate, knowing how to navigate through the delicate issues of your heart. And once you're healed, you will be free to love people in a deeper way than you ever have before.

One of the sad realities of living in our own woundedness is that we tend to cause the very same wounds in others. Hurting people hurt people. Jesus said it this way, "Out of the abundance of the heart the mouth speaks." We have the power of life and death in our tongues, and if we are carrying the death of past hurts with us, what do you think is coming out of our mouths? That's right, death. And it is being poured out on the very ones we love, contributing to the difficulties they'll have to work through in their lives.

I know you're committed to working through this process or you never would have made it this far in the book. Let's examine some specific steps you can take to move forward into wholeness.

ᏩᏃ

● ● ●

Exposing Your Wounds

Start by praying and asking the Lord to reveal the wounds He wants to heal in you.

Ask the Lord to use the Galatians 5 toolset to help you identify areas that are not consistently bearing the fruit of the Spirit. Remember, it's not for convicting or condemning you—it's only purpose is to help identify areas where your flesh is working and preventing you from experiencing the life and joy God has for you.

Be ready to extend an extra portion of grace to yourself. Approach this process with the understanding that there were traumatic experiences that you've gone through—many of which happened at an age when you weren't equipped to process them. As a survival mechanism, it's only natural that you may have developed intricate ways of protecting yourself from experiencing additional emotional pain.

Because of these self-defense mechanisms, you may be blind to your own need and have a natural tendency to see the *problems* in others. Prayer will help you take your eyes off what others are/aren't doing and get them on what the Lord is doing in you.

CGEO

Cooperate with the Process

Allow the Lord to begin showing you the problem areas in your relationships.

Remember, the Lord uses hardship and difficulties in our lives to help us. This area is no different. The areas that irritate you the most about the people in your life—especially pertinent in marriages—are more than likely constructed by the Lord to help you get to the root of the wound.

When you ask the Lord to reveal your wounds, you can be sure He will answer. I know this sounds obvious, but I have to admit that after I asked the Lord, I was a little surprised at how quickly He answered me. His answer came in the form of coordinating circumstances that did a great job of touching the sensitive areas in my soul. Initially, I simply reacted to the pain, but then I realized how precise His aim had been. When the Lord answers you, remember to cooperate with Him and connect with what is going on inside you. The circumstances He brings you through will help you to identify the wound from which your behaviors and emotions are emanating.

As this process unfolds, be ready to extend an extra portion of grace to those around you. You can trust the Lord knows what's going on. Chances are, He is the one orchestrating the annoying people in your life to help you identify the areas in your own heart that need a touch from Him.

CR&O

Memories: God's Way of Healing

Years ago I had a dream—I was being insulted and ridiculed by my stepfather. I had just poured milk from a pitcher into a glass and was getting something to eat. My stepfather began calling me names and criticizing how I was getting a drink of milk. I dropped the pitcher and glass. They fell to the floor, and I engaged in a physical altercation with the man. I was victorious and given a pair of boxing gloves as a trophy.

Then the scene changed. I was on an old cobblestone street, bordered by a rock wall that was about 4 feet tall and about 6 inches wide. On top of the wall was a piece of paper with an arrow that pointed to my left. Then time accelerated, and I watched as the paper dried, withered, turned to dust, and was blown away by the wind.

I heard an audible voice say, "Memories are God's way of healing our wounds." At the time I had no idea what it meant. But through the years, as I have gone through the healing process over and over again, I have discovered wisdom in the dream.

Many times I've experienced destructive behavior from those I trusted. As a child, I was doing things that came naturally to a child, consistent with what was considered normal for my age and level of maturity. But the reactions of those around me were hurtful and confusing. As a result, I reacted out of emotion and became successful at conquering situations in my mind— coming up with conclusions that were destructive, yet made sense to my young mind.

For me, the trophy was learning how to fight—and win. I concluded that I didn't need anyone else.

On the path of life, like that cobblestone street, we make decisions about what directions we will go. Over the course of time we may forget why we do what we do. We may be moving in a direction that is destructive or leads away from our true purpose, and we really don't even know why. Those details can get muted or lost over time.

When God created our brains, He gave us the amazing ability to store detailed information that can be retrieved at a later date. Interestingly enough, that is especially true when it comes to traumatic events. There is a chemical process in which painful and traumatic memories are physically stored and locked into the brain. These memories can be compartmentalized and stored in the subconscious.

Memories can remain hidden for years only to resurface when we least expect it. Most of us have experienced this phenomenon to one degree or another. For example, a smell that reminds us of our grandmother's house or some other childhood event. This can be positive or negative.

I believe this is what the Lord was showing me through the dream. There are some events we go through during our childhood we simply do not have the capacity to resolve. There is no framework of understanding to interpret those events. And in most cases, we're not in an environment that is safe. That's why the Lord will store the memory with great detail until we have what we need to process it.

CSEO

A Personal Recollection

As a young pastor, I had just finished Bible school and was serving on staff at a church in California. I was working full time in construction to take care of my family—while in a non-paid, part-time position with the church.

The Lord began speaking to me saying, "There is a way that seems right to a man, but the end is death." As I pressed in to what the Lord was saying, I felt strongly that he was asking me to direct all my attention toward seeking Him.

Since I was the sole breadwinner in my home, I had no resources available to take any time off work. I had no means of providing for my family other than my job, but felt a clarity regarding the word that I had heard.

One day while I was at work, I was sensing the Lord prompting me again in this regard, so I said, "Okay Lord, I will put all of my attention toward seeking you, but you have to make the way."

Within the hour, my boss came up to me and said, "Luke, I am sorry, but we have to let you go. You are one of our best workers, but the nephew of one of the owners is looking for a job, so we need to make room for him."

Needless to say, I wasn't surprised. I packed up my tools and headed home with a strong conviction that my primary responsibility was to seek the way of the Lord.

That season began in November, and by the end of the month, all our money was spent with no money coming in. December was brutal. Our bills were due, our food was gone, and I felt no release to look for work again. I only heard the same word that started the process, "There is a way that seems right to a man, but the end is death."

To say that people were not supportive would be a gross under exaggeration. I was consistently barraged with rebukes and words of correction from my friends, family, and spiritual leaders. I was told I was worse than an unbeliever and denying my faith. I was told that I'd heard God wrong because "where God guides, God provides."

At one point, a concerned believer brought some groceries to my house. Afterward, the person informed me the food was for my wife and children, not me. With all my heart, I was so thankful for their willingness to provide food for my family.

The pressure and tension when I was around other believers were palpable. It was hard for me to rest in the word the Lord had given me, but I was more concerned for my spiritual well-being than I was for my comfort or even for my physical life. I'd asked the Lord if it would be okay if I looked for work with the understanding that he would keep every door closed until my season was done. I sensed the pleasure of the Lord on that request and started the process of looking for a job. Every door I went to was slammed shut.

By the time Christmas came, I was still without work. I also had my fill of the constant rebukes and words of correction of those around me. I went up to the leadership and said, "You are right. Where God guides, God provides. So since He is not providing for me to be here, I am resigning my position and leaving."

The response I received was, "Whoa, wait a minute—we need to pray about this." To be honest with you, by that time I was so fed up with the resistance I'd received, I didn't want to pray with them about anything. The pastor asked if I'd be willing to meet with him to talk about it. I told him that I would be willing to meet with him but didn't think there was really anything to talk about.

Several days later, I met at the pastor's house with him, his wife, and one of the elders. As I sat on his couch, he said, "I know you're here to talk about moving, but we're not going to talk about that." I can tell you that my internal response wasn't pleasant, but since I want to keep this book's rating to PG, I won't include it here.

"As I was praying for you," the pastor said, "I had a vision of a twelve-year-old boy sitting beneath a wooden deck on the top of a hill overlooking a lake. I saw the boy was crying, and I heard him say, *I am never going to trust anyone again.*"

I knew the Lord had shown the pastor a vision of me when I was a boy. What he didn't know was that I grew up in a house on top of a hill overlooking a lake. When I was hurting or trying to escape the dynamics of my family, one of the places I would hide was beneath the wooden deck in front of our house. He had my attention.

When he laid his hand on me to pray, I exploded with weeping. I'm not talking about the hand-me-a-tissue crying, I'm talking about the let's-get-a-mop crying. Something broke inside me, releasing years of bottled-up pain. I sobbed so deeply that I could hardly sit up. But when it was done, I felt like I'd lost 50 pounds.

The pastor and his wife prayed for me, blessed me, and prophesied over my life. Through that time of ministry, we all began to understand why the Lord had brought me through that process. He was breaking a stronghold in my heart that was preventing me from truly trusting Him.

Within the next couple days, the Lord gave me a dream about where I was going to work and that He was going to send someone to offer me a job. Within about a week, I was offered and accepted a job just as I was shown in my dream.

CR80

Be Ready for Your Memories

When I started asking the Lord to heal my heart, He reminded me of events and circumstances in my childhood. Unexpectedly, and without effort, certain memories would come to my mind. At first, I wrestled against it and tried to push the memories aside. Then I realized that specific memory had everything to do with what the Lord was speaking to me about.

So know this: When you ask the Lord to begin showing areas of your heart that need healing, you can expect He'll bring memories to your mind.

Some memories may be very painful. Some may be troubling. Be ready to revisit those events or circumstances with the help of the Holy Spirit.

If you have hurtful memories that are difficult to face, be encouraged. The fact the Lord brought those memories to the surface is a strong indication you're ready to be healed. You are ready to walk through that event and you have what you need. Ask the Lord to help you walk through it so it can't influence you anymore.

ʚ৪ঌ

Look for Destructive Patterns

As soon as you begin identifying areas of pain and/or irritation, invite the Lord to help you see beyond what is happening on the surface. Resist the urge to respond to the stimuli as you have in the past. Quite often, there are destructive relational patterns that have been established that are rooted in your pain.

For Helen and me, the patterns were so predictable that I knew everything each of us was going to say once an argument got started.

One time, Helen and I were trudging through the rut of our destructive diatribe when I had a picture in my mind of a demon handing her a script and me a script. We had rehearsed our parts so well that we didn't even need queues from the demon anymore. The demon would just hand us the script and we'd take it from there—mindlessly opening our mouths and pouring the garbage in the script onto each other. Then we'd storm off to our corners of self-pity.

For me, I think one of the most maddening aspects of the ruts of miscommunication we had created was that nothing we ever said had anything to do with what was truly going on in our hearts. As the Lord started showing me how to identify my wounds, I was able to look past what Helen was saying or doing and pay attention to how I was feeling and what I was believing in that moment.

I'm not going to sugarcoat anything here. This process was extremely difficult for me. The circumstance touching my wound was incredibly painful. In those moments, I couldn't trust my reactions, so I'd do my best to get away from the situation and connect with the Lord while the emotions were still raging. Even though I knew we were in the middle of a destructive pattern of behavior, the emotional intensity made it hard to pull away.

When you experience dynamics that have touched a sensitive area—one that has consistently taken you out of the fruit of the Spirit—try to peaceably conclude your interaction with the circumstance or individual who is provoking the emotional response. This process is best done with an understanding spouse or friend. However, it's often the people closest to us who are the impetus the Lord uses to bring these things into the open.

Once you can get alone with the Lord, I encourage you to write down what you're feeling and what you're thinking. Identify the key thoughts, beliefs, phrases, etc. you're telling yourself in those moments. These insights will be powerful tools when you walk through the healing process.

Helen and I have grown to the place where we can actually help each other walk through these emotional minefields, even when we're the ones the Lord is using to expose things in the other. Initially, it was quite unnerving because it seemed that the very areas I struggled with stirred up the wounds in her and vice versa. Upon deeper examination, we discovered the Lord had truly brought us together for the purpose of bringing those things into the open. It's amazing how precisely the Lord matched our wounds up with each other. Being part of Helen's healing process and her being part of mine have been a tremendous source of healing for both of us.

As Helen and I learned to identify our own wounds, we were able to seek the Lord for healing and extend grace and understanding to each other. But it took years to get to that place in our relationship. The process was painful and filled with mistakes. Speaking from the other side of the process, I can tell you the price we paid to get here was worth it.

That wasn't the case when we started our journey—and it probably won't be the case for many of you. But this one thing I know, God is faithful to honor His word regardless of our circumstances. He will meet you where you are. He is able to work on your behalf, even if no one else is.

There is another companion along this journey who's always with you and will help if you don't allow it to rule you—your body.

CR80

Listening to Your Body

"We need to talk." As soon as I heard Helen say those words my stomach would tighten and I'd start to feel anxious. Because of the historical pattern of our relationship, I knew those were the words that usually precipitated an argument. My body was preparing for it.

The body was created with an awe-inspiring ability to respond to the dynamics of our environment. The brain catalogs and stores millions of bits of information regarding every circumstance we go through. Once this information is logged, it is easily accessed for future reference.

If we're in an environment that our brain classifies as safe, we'll feel relaxed and comfortable. If the brain finds anything within our environment associated with pain or danger, it will release chemicals to heighten awareness, increase adrenaline, and prepare us to fight or run away.

This is truly an amazing function of the brain, but it does bring about some challenges when interpreting the data. The way this storage system works is with the more-is-better approach. When we encounter a traumatic event, our brain takes the raw data and stores anything and everything about the situation—sights, sounds, smells, and whatever our senses can grab. Once it gathers all the information, it stores it in a file folder and places it in the cabinet marked *Warning*.

When we encounter an element of one item associated with that account, the brain delivers the full folder and automatically makes a real-time association between the former and the current event.

So here's my story about that. Helen, the kids and I were driving down the road after a trip to the mall. I was driving and we were talking about various things, having a casual conversation. As I looked up into the rearview mirror to say something to the kids, the van slightly drifted to the edge of the lane. Helen screamed and grabbed the wheel, causing us to veer sharply into the left lane. I quickly grabbed the wheel and got the van under control and back into the right lane.

In reality, we were never in danger. We weren't even close to hitting the shoulder of the road, much less the ditch. We were in more danger from Helen's reaction than we were before her intervention. What happened?

When Helen was in her early 20s, she and her fiancé were traveling home from a party. Unknown to Helen, he was impaired. They'd only made it part of the way home when he missed a corner and crashed into a steel support beam. Her fiancé was killed instantly, and Helen was thrown through the windshield. Sustaining numerous life-threatening injuries, she was in a coma for several days. With years of therapy—and even several miracles— she fully recovered. Physically.

Over a quarter of a century later, when we're driving down the road and the car starts to drift, her brain immediately recognizes this minor detail as one of the data points in the file folder belonging to that prior accident. Her brain brings the emotions, along with the appropriate chemicals, into the moment so she can respond quickly to the danger and preserve her life.

This process is repeated multiple times in our lives on a daily basis. Our brain is trained to minimize the need for completely reanalyzing every situation from scratch. Instead, it pulls from past experiences and fills the gaps for us. That's helpful as long as our historical files are based on good information.

Now let's get back to Helen telling me that we needed to talk. Why would I be nervous? Why would my stomach start to tighten? Because that phrase was associated with a folder containing details of events that were extremely painful for me.

As the Lord healed me and brought me back to the original folders of information, two things happened. One, of course, was that I was able to purge the file of unnecessary information and re-catalog some things. The other was surprising to me.

I discovered the anxiety I was feeling from the past event actually influenced the outcome of the current event. Because I was nervous and experiencing the emotional-chemical cocktail of my past hurts, I was interjecting it into the conversation with Helen. Intuitively, she could read my body language and that helped to remind her brain of previous conversations that all ended badly. This cycle that started by the association of one thing ended up reinforcing the previous information stored in the brain.

Armed with this knowledge, Helen and I have trained ourselves to read our own body language in these types of situations. Dry mouth, anxious feelings, sweating, stomach pain—for us, these are all part of the vocabulary our bodies use to communicate that something else is going on beyond the reality of the current circumstance.

Helen's body talks to her differently than mine does to me. Each of us has to learn how our body responds to the world around us. As we do, it will become another tool to help recognize the things that have been preventing us from fully experiencing the freedom available to us in the Lord.

There are times my body knows something is out of place before I do. I've learned to pay attention to how I feel. Sometimes I'll realize that I am feeling anxious, but I don't even know why. Once I become aware, I simply ask the Lord, "Why am I feeling anxious?" As I quiet myself before Him, He usually lets me know right away. Other times, I'll tell Helen what I'm feeling and ask her to pray for me. One way or the other, the Lord always reveals what is going on and helps us sort it out.

So pay attention to the clues your body is sending you. The next time you're in an unpleasant situation, make note of how your body responds. That will help you identify potential issues from the past as well as help sort out what is going on in the present.

Learning to identify your wounds and issues of your past is a critical step in the healing process—but it's just a step. There is a journey in front of you, and you'll need to know what to do with what He is showing you. The next chapter maps out some preparation steps for that journey.

CB&O

Chapter 12

Practical Steps: Preparation

You've covered a lot of groundwork. You've learned to recognize the dynamic interaction between your wounds and the world around you. You know how to identify behaviors and emotions empowered by the flesh. Now you're ready to take practical steps that move you into the healing available in Christ.

In this next section I'll be referencing and expanding on content we've already covered. The dynamics of the emotional and spiritual subjects that we've covered generally will now be looked at personally, specifically. Up to this point, we've been skimming the surface of your heart. I intentionally wrote about tender areas in a way that would be relatively impersonal. But moving forward, it's time to make it personal.

ᝏᝏ

Be Prepared

To a degree, the word *preparation* is a misnomer for what you're about to undergo. Your journey to healing will be unique to you. Only the Lord truly knows the process you'll need to go through so you can get where you're going.

That being said, you can prepare your heart to visit the areas needing to be healed. Most of these are common sense, and I don't mean to sound condescending in any way. For me, it has been the simple and obvious things that I've held on to through some of the most difficult times in my life, including the process of getting free from my pain.

Be Ready and Willing to Change and Grow

I believe you already are committed to this. But there is another level of intentionality that will help prepare you for what's coming. The willingness to move into situations where you're expecting change can become a powerful, stabilizing force in the face of uncertainty.

Positioning yourself for transformation starts with recognizing and acknowledging that something in you needs to change. Something isn't the way it's supposed to be.

It took me two failed marriages and numerous broken relationships to acknowledge I was the problem—or at least a major contributor to the problems—in the relational dynamics of my life. Admitting I needed to change was a critical first step, even though at that moment I had no idea what that change was.

This mindset also prepares you for the fact you're going to change. You and I have a natural resistance to change, even good change. Part of us wants that predictability and wants the world to change around us, but fitting into our expectation of what it should be. Being mentally ready and willing to change sets our expectation to anticipate change—and change we must, if we're going to move beyond the ruts of destructive behavior. The expectation of change gives us courage to press into areas we've not ventured into before.

When I realized my arguing with Helen was a predictable pattern, it was like reading a script. I forced myself to change my response. I'm not suggesting I responded better or worse. I just refused to accept the old patterns that I knew were destructive. Instead of taking my queue and delivering my line, I'd walk away and slam the door. Or instead of defending my point, I'd say, "I can see how you might think that way."

Initially, I was more concerned with disrupting the predictable and familiar behaviors than I was with making sure I was doing everything right. I knew if I didn't start moving away from where I was, I'd stay trapped in the same old patterns.

Be Willing to Fail

Without failure, you'll remain trapped in your current condition. When you're learning something new, recognize that failure is a natural part of the process. Give yourself permission to learn, grow, and make mistakes in the process. Allow your heart to walk in freedom and wholeness—and please the Lord with your life. Failure can be a stumbling block or a steppingstone, depending on how you choose to view it.

This Is Gonna Hurt

I know that goes without saying, but nevertheless, there it is. The journey you're on will lead you right back into the moments of your deepest pain.

I've been amazed at how accurately the pain of my past has been replicated in the moments just prior to my healing. On many occasions, I'd felt like I was in the very place and time that the wound took place. The difference was that this time I knew the Lord was with me to break its power in my life.

Pain is going to be part of the process, but it's a small price to pay for a life of freedom from the past.

Decrease the Dosage

If you've been medicating your pain, I recommend decreasing the dose. If you feel you can, stop it all together. I'm talking specifically about those things that you're looking to that are designed to keep you from experiencing the emotional impact of past hurts.

Getting to the heart of the pain often takes getting rid of the substances, relationships, or behaviors you've employed to bury it.

I know this is frightening for many people. It was for me as well. This is where your courage and confidence in the Lord need to kick in. The fear and pain of your wounds need to be exposed to the air and the light in order to heal. It's difficult for that to happen if they're covered beneath the fog of your attempts to medicate them.

Let me be clear. When you decrease or stop medicating your pain, those pain levels will increase. The lies, hurt, and confusion of your past won't be suppressed—they'll bubble to the surface. That's a good thing. It's exactly what you need to start getting to the heart of the matter. You can be sure the Holy Spirit will help you through the process of healing.

If you don't feel you have the strength to stop medicating your pain, keep moving forward with the process of healing anyway. There may be times it feels like too much and you don't know how to depend on the Lord for relief. It's more important to work with the Lord as you feel able than to abandon the effort. The Lord is not angry or disappointed with you. He is for you and will walk with you through this process, regardless of your starting point.

Here is the hope I can share with you. Regardless of what you have used in the past to medicate your pain, you won't need it once the wound has been healed.

Recognize the Process

I use the words *journey* and *process* to convey the fact that there will be a period of time for the healing to take place. In my case, that journey lasted many years. The first leg of the journey was the most difficult since I didn't know any of the things I'm sharing with you in this book. It was also more intense at the beginning because the Lord went directly to the deepest areas of pain.

Once those deep wounds were healed, the Lord brought me through a number of other seasons of exposing less painful areas. They were challenging at times, but the intensity was much less than at first. That's because two things were happening simultaneously. Firstly, I was healed of the deepest wounds. That changed how I related to everything and everyone. Secondly, I was learning more about God's love and faithfulness toward me. Not only was I losing the fear of going through the healing process, I started looking forward to it.

Think of the process as a medical intervention. If you were run over by a truck and your heart stopped, the paramedics aren't going to set your broken leg. They'll address the critical areas first. That's how the Lord works with us. I think I'd have preferred He started with some easy stuff and worked His way to the more difficult, but it was the exact opposite for me.

In retrospect, I'm so glad He did it the way He did. The big stuff gets out of the way up front—the rest is addressed on an as-needed basis.

Don't Travel Alone

This can be a tough one, depending on your circumstances. At the beginning of this process, you might be surrounded with people who are wrapped up in and even part of perpetuating the destructive cycles in your life.

If you're part of a strong, Bible-believing community, then reach out and connect with mature believers who can help you walk through the process—even if they're just there to encourage you or pray for you. There are a growing number of churches and ministries that are learning about these types of healing tools.

If you don't feel you have anyone who can go through this process with you, don't be discouraged. Whether you have other people or not, you have the Holy Spirit who will help and encourage you through the process.

* * *

For the first part of my journey, I was alone. I had one or two friends who I could call and ask for prayer, but for the most part, it was just the Holy Spirit and me. I don't recommend doing this journey alone if you have another option.

If you don't have anyone who can help lead you through the process, find others who you can help walk through theirs. If God is your Father and you're in the process of growing with Him, you have something to share with others around you.

In my marriage with Helen, I went through the process of healing and learning these things first. When I received revelation, I shared it with her. As I began walking in greater levels of freedom, she could see the fruit in my life and the impact in our relationship. Then she started applying them in her life. I made a lot of mistakes and it wasn't easy—for either of us. But as a result, Helen and I have become our own greatest support team. I help her and she helps me.

If you're not married or don't have a spouse who is ready to take the journey with you, I would recommend connecting with other believers who are committed to growing in Christ and learning the process with you.

You and I weren't designed to live as emotional islands. We were created to live in fellowship with others. We were created to live interdependently with others. Not independent, and not co-dependent, but interdependent.

Don't Hesitate to Get Help

There may very well be times and seasons where you'll need professional help to navigate the complexities of dealing with certain traumatic events in your past. That is nothing to be ashamed about—and in fact, it's a sign of wisdom. Even if you need to pay for help, it will be money well spent. As I've shared, there were areas where I sought help from a professional—and I've never regretted the decision to do so.

There are events and circumstances we need to go through that we're not equipped to go alone. This is by design. Sometimes the Lord puts a weight in front of us so we can't lift it without the help of others. When those times come, ask for help. Do what you need to do to get the help you need—whether it's a pastor, counselor, or medical professional.

When seeking help, look for someone who understands the three realms of your identity—you are a spirit, soul, and body. Seek someone who understands that some issues are connected to spiritual issues that may have demonic influence. Be sure the person can help equip and empower you to walk victoriously—as opposed to someone who tries to teach you to cope with your issues.

The tools and principles shared in this book have been critical components of the restoration work in my wife's life and mine. But there was a season where we both had to get help outside of ourselves and outside of the church.

I knew that the Lord had brought Helen and me together when we met. To this day, I've never doubted that—even though our relationship has been tested to the extreme.

I've loved her dearly and always thought of her as my best friend. But I just couldn't understand why it was impossible to reason with her when we disagreed.

When we were married, Helen had two boys, and I had two boys and a girl. Her sons were 13 and 15. My sons were 15 and 21, and my daughter was 19. My two older children lived on their own; I shared custody of my youngest with his mother. There were many subtle complexities of our blended family, but these dynamics mixed with our wounded hearts were a recipe for conflict. That conflict would result in an event that would shake our family to the core.

There were a number of contributing factors that set us up for a challenging situation. Helen and her boys are Brazilian. She'd been widowed, raising the two boys on her own for about five years. I'm an American, had been divorced, working on co-raising my children with their mother and stepfather. Even in a best-case scenario with two well-adjusted, healthy individuals, these dynamics would be difficult. But this wasn't a best-case scenario—and we were neither well-adjusted nor healthy, which we soon found out.

The first leg of our journey together was filled with precious times of connecting and explosive times of conflict. Conflicts that began as heated arguments when we were first married had escalated to screaming matches, which included slamming doors, punching walls, and flipping furniture around the house.

One afternoon—late in October 2005, we'd been married for about ten months—Helen and I were having a discussion upstairs while the boys were playing downstairs. Helen made a comment, and I immediately reacted by pushing her. Before I could even think, she was on the floor. I was shocked, ashamed, and gripped with fear.

I'd never acted out like that before, and it frightened me that I'd acted so quickly and violently without even thinking. I knew something was dreadfully wrong. The next day I started calling around for a Christian counselor. I found one and scheduled my first session.

Over the next several weeks, my counselor helped me identify some key issues that were driving forces behind my behavior. There were a number of traumatic events throughout my childhood that had produced a form of PTSD (Post Traumatic Stress Disorder). The dynamics of my marriage at the time were tapping in to these events and causing an intense release of emotions directed toward my wife.

In November, I had just gone through a healing therapy session with my counselor, who is a Certified Trauma Counselor. The session was deeply painful and emotional and had left me exhausted and emotionally raw.

That night, after Helen and I had gone to bed, I made a comment that offended her and she began a verbal attack. At that point, I just wanted her to get away from me, so I turned sideways in the bed and pushed her out with my feet. She fell on the floor and immediately grabbed the phone and called 911.

I quickly jumped out of bed and tried to grab the phone to hang it up. She held tightly and we began to wrestle over the phone. I jerked it away from the wall and broke the line. The room was dark and the momentum of my pulling away from the wall pushed us both toward our walk-in closet. My foot caught the edge of the opening and I tripped, falling on top of Helen.

She didn't know I tripped, so from her perspective she thought I had intentionally thrown her on the ground. I stood her up and pushed her against the shelves in the closet. She began to hit me and scream, "Just kill me! Just kill me!"

With one hand, I held her back and blocked her hands with the other. Then I heard the phone ring. I knew what came next. I got dressed and waited for the police to arrive.

The whole ordeal took place in about 30 seconds, but the impact of that moment took years to work through.

On November 11, 2005, I was arrested and charged with false imprisonment, domestic abuse, and disorderly conduct. That was the last time I saw Helen for three months.

During those three months, I met twice a week with my counselor who helped me work through the emotional and spiritual issues surrounding these events and the events of my past. I cannot begin to imagine being able to navigate the complexities of the emotional pain in my heart without the help of a professional.

So if you're finding it difficult to work through events of your past—events hindering you from experiencing fullness of life today—don't hesitate to seek help. Personally, I recommend finding a counselor who is a Spirit-filled, solution-focused Christian.

Invest in Understanding God's Love

Ask almost anyone and they'll tell you that they know God loves them. They know He loves the world and sent His Son to demonstrate His love once and for all. However, I'd argue that when it really comes down to it, very few people are really and truly convinced He loves them as an individual.

There are subtle ideas interwoven within our beliefs. They are simple words, like *if* and *when*. God loves me if I do what's right. If I read the Bible and pray. When I'm good. When I don't do [fill in the blank with a sin you've struggled with].

God's love for you and commitment to you are far beyond your ability to comprehend. There are timeless and profoundly specific promises you can review to remind yourself of this. I recommend doing it often.

For God so loved the world, that He gave His only begotten Son, that whoever believes in Him shall not perish, but have eternal life. For God did not send the Son into the world to judge the world, but that the world might be saved through Him. (John 3:16-17)

But God demonstrates His own love toward us, in that while we were yet sinners, Christ died for us. (Romans 5:8)

"For I know the plans that I have for you," declares the Lord, "plans for welfare and not for calamity to give you a future and a hope. Then you will call upon Me and come and pray to Me, and I will listen to you." (Jeremiah 29:11-12)

For I am confident of this very thing, that He who began a good work in you will perfect it until the day of Christ Jesus. (Philippians 1:6)

Beloved, you are a new creation in Christ. The old is gone, and you are in a new season. You have already been reconciled to God—He's not holding your sins against you. Jesus Christ bore your sin so you could have right standing with God! The payment and penalty for anything you have or have not done has been paid in full.

Therefore if anyone is in Christ, he is a new creature; the old things passed away; behold, new things have come. Now all these things are from God, who reconciled us to Himself through Christ and gave us the ministry of reconciliation, namely, that God was in Christ reconciling the world to Himself, not counting their trespasses against them, and He has committed to us the word of reconciliation. (2 Corinthians 5:17-19)

Committing these truths to memory is an explosively powerful weapon you can use to demolish the lies that will come at you throughout this journey.

Fix Your Eyes

We're admonished to fix our eyes on our example, Jesus Christ, as we pursue the prize before us—the high calling of God.

Therefore, since we have so great a cloud of witnesses surrounding us, let us also lay aside every encumbrance and the sin which so easily entangles us, and let us run with endurance the race that is set before us, fixing our eyes on Jesus, the author and perfecter of faith, who for the joy set before Him endured the cross, despising the shame, and has sat down at the right hand of the throne of God. For consider Him who has endured such hostility by sinners against Himself, so that you will not grow weary and lose heart. (Hebrews 12:1-3)

This process includes laying aside things that may slow us down. It also includes a call to endurance, seeing the process as a race set before us. We've looked at passages previously that discussed following Jesus' example of His willingness to suffer for the sake of the kingdom. These are all valid and encouraging.

There is something unique about this Hebrews 12 passage because it reveals a key Jesus used to find the strength to endure. He looked beyond the pain of the process to the reward on the other side of it. The joy set before Him became the focal point of His attention as He passed through the Garden of Gethsemane, down the way of suffering, to His crucifixion and death.

What was the joy He was gazing upon that held Him through this process?

These things I have spoken to you so that My joy may be in you, and that your joy may be made full. (John 15:11)

You and I, along with our brothers and sisters throughout history and throughout the world, are the reward of Jesus' suffering. We are His joy. Through His pain, Jesus' thoughts were on us—as well as on the fellowship He was establishing through us. The wounds, bruises, and stripes He bore removed anything that could separate us from His love.

The text in Hebrews encourages us to "fix our eyes on Jesus." This wasn't just for the sake of understanding His example. It was to understand the other side of our savior's gaze. He was looking to us, His joy. So now we can look beyond the pain of our process and know that it is working to bring us into the fullness of joy in our unhindered fellowship with Him. Our joy is being made full.

What we will go through cannot compare to the beauty and joy that will be the outcome.

For I consider that the sufferings of this present time are not worthy to be compared with the glory that is to be revealed to us. (Romans 8:18)

For momentary, light affliction is producing for us an eternal weight of glory far beyond all comparison. (2 Corinthians 4:17)

Arming ourselves with the truth gives us something solid to hold on to when our thoughts and feelings begin to swirl around the wounds that are exposed.

Here are a few lies I was told as I was walking through my process.

God hates you and has rejected you. You have failed so many times that He doesn't even hear you when you ask for forgiveness. You will never be able to break out of this behavior. Why would God want someone like you? Why would God ever want you to share His Word with anyone, you can't even live it yourself.

Like flies swarming out of a rotting garbage can, the lies of the enemy spewed out into my conscious mind when I opened up the festering wounds of my heart. If I hadn't prepared myself with the truth before opening these dark places in my belief systems, I would have probably just shut the lid and tried to hide it again. Instead I began capturing the flies and crushing them with the truth.

God's Word is the most amazing tool available to us in this process. Learning God's Word takes time and effort—well worth it regardless of the cost. Check out the appendix section of this book for a convenient, scripture-based list of who you are in Him.

But Scripture isn't the only resource available. There is another tool that takes absolutely no effort on your part, but if you're like me, it can be one of the hardest things you'll learn to do . . . or should I say, not do.

C♋ಎ

Chapter 13

Engaging the Holy Spirit

On your journey, you'll need a guide. Not just any guide—one who's been where you are going and knows how to get you through to your ultimate destination. The Holy Spirit is that guide.

The Holy Spirit is your Helper. He is the One who has been called alongside you to bring you into the fullness of everything that was purchased through the death, burial, and resurrection of Jesus Christ. The Holy Spirit is your guide. He is your support. He is your comforter—and you will need Him every step of the journey.

The truth is, you wouldn't even be able to have a relationship with God without the Holy Spirit. You couldn't perceive your need for salvation without Him. You wouldn't be able to understand the Word of God without Him. He is constantly working in you and with you in every aspect of your relationship with the Father. I'm stating that emphatically to call attention to this: Although He saturates every fiber of your existence in Christ—whether you are aware of it or not—the Holy Spirit desires a personal relationship with you.

As you acknowledge and engage the Holy Spirit through your walk with the Lord, He will reveal Jesus Christ and His provision for you in this process. In John 16, Jesus spoke of the Father's plan to send the Holy Spirit.

I have many more things to say to you, but you cannot bear them now. But when He, the Spirit of truth, comes, He will guide you into all the truth; for He will not speak on His own initiative, but whatever He hears, He will speak; and He will disclose to you what is to come. He will glorify Me, for He will take of Mine and will disclose it to you. All things that the Father has are Mine; therefore I said that He takes of Mine and will disclose it to you. (John 16:12-15)

The Holy Spirit guides you, reveals truth, and exposes your heart to the loving provision that has been made available to you. I encourage you to engage frequently with the Helper. He is always with you and will direct and strengthen you to enter into the freedom and wholeness that is already yours in Christ Jesus.

Now may the God of hope fill you with all joy and peace in believing, so that you will abound in hope by the power of the Holy Spirit. (Romans 15:13)

CR80

Be Still

My life was in shambles. My marriage, ministry, and business were in ruins. And I was being tormented with thoughts of suicide. Even though some of the mess was due to things outside my control, most of it was a direct result of my own destructive decisions. The outcome of my choices was obvious, but I was having a hard time determining what exactly it was that I was doing that resulted in such chaos.

It wasn't that I was involved with overtly sinful behavior—those issues are easier to identify. For the most part, I was trying to live a godly life and hold on to things that would be palatable by most religious standards. But even though the external behaviors were in check, I knew what was going on inside me wasn't consistent with the abundant life of righteousness, peace, and joy in the Holy Spirit that is promised to believers in Scripture.

It was a moment in my life where I came to an end. It was an end to a part of me that I had tried so hard to tame and train. It was a part of me that struggled with self-reliance, lust, bitterness, and hate. A part of me that I kept buried and subdued. A part that drained my energy and warred against my heart's desire to live for the Lord. It was in this moment that I opened every door to the darkest, most painful, and most embarrassing areas of my heart. In that place, through tear-filled eyes, I pleaded with the Lord to do whatever He had to do to set me free.

He heard me.

I was ready to receive whatever consequence, whatever pain or punishment necessary—I just had to be free. I couldn't continue to live a life outside of what I knew was available to me in Him. I braced myself and His answer came.

"Come before me and be still." That was where the journey began. A call to silence. A call to wait.

At first it seemed almost impossible to quiet the raging storm of thoughts and feelings. *I'm wasting my time! This is ridiculous! This can't be the Lord—I should be praying or reading the Bible or studying.*

The thoughts crashed against me like waves, but the Lord had given me a verse, calling me to be still and know that He is God.

I fixed my awareness on the simple reality that *He is God.* Whenever a thought would try to come to mind—a concern, an argument, a distraction—my response was to simply realign my awareness to the reality that *He is God.*

I began to realize the significance of that one revelation, *He is God.* Regardless of the challenge, problem, difficulty, or task, everything had to be confronted with the reality that the one I serve is God. He is God over everything. He is the God who knows everything. He is the God of all power, authority, and might. And He is the God who loves me.

What I discovered is the things that overwhelmed me weren't as big as I thought they were. Instead of viewing those things in comparison to my abilities, I started comparing them to the character and characteristics of God as revealed by His various names.

What about the strife and the stress? He is Jehovah-Shalom, the God of peace.

But what about the wounds and pain? He is Jehovah-Rapha, the Lord, your healer.

And when I feel alone? He is Jehovah-Shammah, the Lord is there.

But I am confused and don't know what to do. Yes, but He is Jehovah-Rohi, the Lord my Shepherd.

I started to build a wall around my time of stillness before the Lord. Each stone had a name of the Lord etched on it. There was no worry, no fear, no concern that could overcome the reality that nothing could compare to my God. In that place of awareness, I rested. In that place I heard the still small voice say, "Invite me into your pain."

CR80

Invite the Holy Spirit into the Darkness

The next thing the Lord spoke to me crashed against my religious mind like a sledgehammer.

During that season of my life, I'd frequently be overwhelmed with intense emotions. Someone would say or do something, and immediately my emotions would spike. Sometimes anger, sometimes rage, sometimes hate would fill me. I tried to fight against the thoughts and worked to suppress my emotions from showing. Like a nonstop battle to hold a beach ball under water, the pressure was constant. But I'd learned to hold them down—at least until something triggered me. When the pressure became too much to hold, my pain would gush out on to those around me. I was exhausted. Yet each time I'd re-exert myself to do what needed to be done.

Then I heard the Lord say, "Don't bury it, invite me into it."

My thoughts and feelings were so ugly. So ungodly. In some cases, they were downright evil. I'd been trained by religion that I needed to be good if I wanted the good things of God in my life. In my mind, those thoughts and behaviors made me unacceptable to the Lord. I had to keep them under control to stay in His presence. I'd actually thought the devil was my problem, the one behind the darkness in my life. Why would the Lord want me to invite Him into the things that would give Him the right to reject me?

In spite of my questions, I obeyed the voice of the Lord. Every time those emotions overtook me, I'd go before Him and ask Him to come in. Come in to my hatred. Come in to my rage. Come in to my lust. Come in to my fear. Come in to my doubt and disbelief.

In the days and weeks that followed, I'd started having flashes of memories from the dark and painful times of my past. At first I tried to suppress them, shut them out. Then I realized the Lord was bringing me to those places intentionally. The memories He brought to my attention were at the root of the emotions I was experiencing.

As a result, He navigated through the ugliness to the root of my pain. It was in those places where He brought correction, insight, and healing.

The light is not intimidated by the darkness. God's righteousness is not affected by sin. God's love is not only able to reach into the deepest, darkest areas of the heart, it's able to transform the heart.

But all things become visible when they are exposed by the light, for everything that becomes visible is light. (Ephesians 5:13)

There is no evil so great that it can resist God's ability to redeem and transform. There are no wounds beyond His ability to heal. There is nothing broken beyond His ability to restore. Everything you bring to Him, no matter how dark, will become light when Christ shines on it.

Ask the Holy Spirit to help you! God longs to heal you. He longs to have deeper fellowship with you. It's His will and desire for you to be free, whole, and joyful. He is totally committed to you—no matter what.

∞

Remove Restrictions

There is a direct correlation between your willingness to trust the Lord and the freedom you will find.

The Lord isn't withholding anything from you—you are the one who holds the authority to decide what you allow God to do in your life. Because of your free will, the Lord will never violate your decision regarding His work in your life. By giving you free will, the Lord has chosen to limit His ability to work in you to the extent of your willingness to allow Him.

I have observed—in my life and in the lives of others I've worked with—substantial increase in the evidence of the working of the Lord in those who willingly surrendered to His process without restriction. Although there are slight variations, this is the statement I hear: "Lord, do whatever you need to do . . . "

My regular prayer before the Lord goes like this: "Holy Spirit, do whatever you need to do so that I may walk in the fullness of everything that was purchased for me through the death and resurrection of Jesus Christ."

That's not something to enter into lightly. Remember, you've probably spent your life building a framework of beliefs and behaviors designed to protect you from harm and painful feelings. When you remove the restrictions, you're letting the Lord know you trust Him to lead you into those places of pain. You can be sure that is exactly where He will take you.

It's not something to fear. Even though you may have trained yourself to fear hurt and avoid pain, the reality is that fear and pain are often doors leading to your promise. The Lord will lead you to these places so you can pass through them. They are not the destination—they are mere obstacles obscuring the view of your identity and destiny in Christ.

When you begin trusting in God's goodness and realizing His amazing love for you, you will have the courage to face the darkness of the unknown places in your heart. Hold tightly to the truth of His loving-kindness, and it will guide you to, through, and beyond the wounds and lies at the heart of your fears.

As you remove the restrictions from the Lord, you'll also need to begin minimizing your reliance on anything other than Him for comfort or security.

Learning to engage with the Holy Spirit to navigate the healing journey is vital for victory. He will teach you the truth and help you separate the precious from the worthless. One of the important steps in this process is to consider the beliefs and paradigms that can get in the way.

CREX

Chapter 14

Paradigms that May Hinder

Keeping your focus is critical on this journey. Your perception of what you see is equally important. There are some perspectives that can cause you unnecessary difficulty on your journey to wholeness—you'll need to avoid them.

In my walk with the Lord and my journey of restoration, I've encountered a number of belief systems in the church that I recommend avoiding. For me, they were not only unhelpful, they were a hindrance to the work of the Spirit in my life.

☙❧

Dealing with the Past

One day I was discussing the passage in 2 Corinthians 5:17 that states that we are a new creation in Christ and that the old has passed away and the new has come. The topic came up because I had heard a popular pastor mention that he didn't believe in inner healing, counseling, or anything to do with the things in our past. He used this passage to support his assumptions.

This was in direct contradiction to the process the Lord was working in me. When I'd asked the Lord about it, this is what I heard: "If it was truly in your past, would it still be affecting you today?"

Through that revelation, I felt at liberty to address whatever the Lord brought up to me, whether from my past or present. When something is affecting your relationships today, it isn't in your past. The wound may have initially happened in your past, but it's affecting your present.

I believe I am a new creation. My past is dead and buried—and all my sin has been forgiven. There is nothing there for me to find. That being said, although I don't dig around in my past, I don't ignore when the Lord brings something to mind.

My eyes are looking forward. I am pressing on to the mark of God's high calling in Christ Jesus. If something from my past—or present, for that matter—blocks my view, I address it. And then, I move on—eyes forward.

CRORO

The Extremes

There are two potential extremes regarding the spiritual nature of dealing with hurts and hardships. One is to demonize them, and the other is to accept everything as being God's will. Neither of these extremes is true. Holding to one or the other can prevent you from finding the healing and freedom that belong to you in Christ.

There are some who ascribe any hardship as being from the devil. From this perspective, we're encouraged to reject anything that may cause pain, discomfort, or expose the working of evil in our lives. This paradigm can cause a destructive focus on the demonic realm and the activity of the enemy.

Even though it's important to be aware of areas where the enemy may try to take advantage or cause a stumbling block, you don't need to go looking for demons hiding behind every bush. I don't look for what the enemy is doing—I keep my eyes focused on what the Lord is doing. When the enemy tries to hinder me from moving forward into what the Lord has for me, that's when he reveals himself. When he is exposed, I deal with him accordingly, get him out of my way, and proceed on my path toward the Lord.

On the other side of the spectrum, I've seen some people who willingly accept any kind of garbage or abuse, thinking God expects them to just accept it as His will. To be sure, you and I will suffer hardship—and even persecution—in this world, which we've discussed. But that doesn't mean we have to accept all sorrow, sickness, disease, and suffering. In Isaiah 53, we see that Jesus paid a high price for our healing, wholeness, and peace.

Surely our griefs He Himself bore, and our sorrows He carried; yet we ourselves esteemed Him stricken, smitten of God, and afflicted. But He was pierced through for our transgressions, He was crushed for our iniquities; the chastening for our well-being fell upon Him, and by His scourging we are healed. All of us like sheep have gone astray, each of us has turned to his own way; but the Lord has caused the iniquity of us all to fall on Him. (Isaiah 53:4-6)

Jesus bore the full weight of suffering for your soul and body. You're not relegated to a life of physical or emotional pain because of the price He paid for you.

I admit there are things about this full payment I don't understand. There are some people who suffer physical and psychological pains that are not healed or completely restored. My father was a believer, yet he died with cancer. On the other hand, I've seen God miraculously heal people who weren't even saved. These things I don't understand and make no attempt to explain them.

What I do know is that my lack of understanding doesn't invalidate the truth. Nor does my understanding verify it. There are many things beyond my ability to comprehend, much less understand. Yet, I stand firm on what God says in His Word. And when I don't understand, I trust His love and kind intention toward me.

• • •

If you avoid extreme teachings and place your trust in the Lord, He will navigate you through the valley of what's in between.

CRBO

Fear of Failure

At the beginning of my journey, I was crippled by a fear of failure. In my mind, failing would confirm my fear that I was a failure. So I'd only do things giving me a high-level assurance of success.

When I was a young father, the Lord often used my relationship with my children to reveal Himself to me. One day He reminded me of when my children were learning to walk. He asked me, "How did you respond when your children took their first few steps and then fell? Did you spank them for falling?"

"Of course not, Lord!" I said. "I celebrated their first steps."

"Then why would you think that is how I would treat you?"

The standard I had for myself was that I had to be perfect to be acceptable. I believed failure was my enemy, so I did everything to avoid it. When I failed—whether it was giving in to sinful behavior or falling short of an expected outcome—I'd mentally punish myself for days.

When the Lord opened my eyes to His heart toward me, which was as a Father walking through his child's growth process, my perspective started to shift. Instead of living under the pressure to measure up, I understood I was a child learning to walk in a new expression of my faith.

Failure is not my enemy—without it I couldn't grow.

If you're not failing, you're not growing. If you're not failing, you will never reach the potential of being who God created you to be.

When my behavior would step outside of what I knew to be acceptable before the Lord, I would confess it as sin and agree I didn't want that behavior to be a part of my walk with Him. I would receive the Lord's forgiveness and the righteousness He provided for me. Then I would thank Him for His promise to cleanse me of all unrighteousness.

If we confess our sins, He is faithful and righteous to forgive us our sins and to cleanse us from all unrighteousness. (1 John 1:9)

From that point on, I wouldn't allow myself to feel guilt, shame, or condemnation—which had previously been the tools I'd use to punish myself.

CৰৎৎO

God Is Mad at You

The truth: God is not mad at you. Let me just say right off the bat, it is impossible for God to be mad at you for your sin. That may seem like a bold statement, but to believe anything else is to contradict the message of the cross of Jesus Christ.

When Jesus took the sin of the world upon Himself, He bore the wrath of God for sin. He fully paid the just penalty for sin by His death. The case against us that had been presented through the Law was addressed at every point by the life and death of our Savior.

Not only is He not mad at you for your past, He will not be mad at you if you sin, fail, make a mistake, etc. Some religious folks get real nervous when I make this statement. They're afraid that if we don't scare people into obedience, believers will run off into all kinds of sinful behavior to whatever horrible end.

God's Word is clear. Romans 2:4 says "the kindness of God leads you to repentance." It's the revelation of His love that compels our hearts to seek Him.

There is a severity to the Lord as we discussed earlier. I have no misgivings about that. And I can agree wholeheartedly that there is a reverential fear of the Lord that drives me toward wisdom. These realities have nothing to do with believing God is angry with me. Far from it.

The Lord's discipline and correction are clear indicators of His love and commitment to my development—never are they an expression of anger.

The lie that God was mad at me or would be mad at me if I failed to meet His expectations was paralyzing my relationship with Him. It crippled me from growing because I was afraid of making a mistake. How could I step into something new without the possibility of failure? How could I be perfect when I'm trapped inside a vessel that loves sin and the world and will cooperate with the enemy of my soul at every turn?

As a believer, anger isn't part of your relationship with the Lord. He has removed your sin and freely given you His righteousness. You are in His Son, and the Father is pleased with Him.

This doesn't change the fact that your choices may sow seeds that will bring about a bitter harvest. That is simply the manifestation of the reaping-and-sowing principle. It has nothing to do with how God feels about you. He is not mad at you. He loves you. He is for you. You are His child.

∞

You Have to be Good to be Accepted

The flipside of the belief that God is mad at you is the idea that you have to be good in order for Him to accept you. Good is a relative term. From God's perspective, any definition of good that involves something we do falls woefully short of His standard.

God's definition of good is Jesus Christ. There is nothing you can add to Him. Your deeds are not required. You were declared righteous. It was imputed, that is to say, it was accredited to you apart from your involvement. You are already completely accepted into God's beloved Son.

To say you have to do something to be good enough for God is to say the price Jesus paid for you wasn't enough. That would be the pinnacle of arrogance, wouldn't it?

Grasp the truth that there is nothing you can do to add or subtract from the value God has ascribed to you. His love and acceptance of you were initiated and completed by Him—apart from your contribution. You can accept it. You can reject it. But that is the full extent of your part in this matter.

Sadly, religious culture holds to the deception that a believer's value and acceptance by the Lord are somehow tied to behavior—for good or ill. Please divorce yourself from that mentality and fully embrace the cross as the complete payment for your sin. Acknowledge the Spirit of life in Christ Jesus as the full measure of your righteousness.

You are completely forgiven of sins—past, present, and future. You are completely righteous because Jesus Christ fulfilled everything you couldn't do and made you one with Himself. You have the Holy Spirit, who was given to teach and enable you to walk in what has already been accomplished for you.

The path before you is simply the process of bringing your thoughts and beliefs into agreement with who God says you already are in Him. Regularly reading and meditating on Romans 8 will help to establish this in your heart.

ೞೠ

Silence

There is a deadly silence covering many congregations. It's a silence regarding sin. It's not that people aren't speaking against sin—it's when they do, it belongs to someone else. This silence has given the enemy an incredible amount of room to creep in and out of people's lives and release his purposes in individuals and congregations.

God's Word instructs believers to confess our sins to one another. That's an area where we have fallen short, keeping silent when we really needed to speak out.

I certainly support addressing sin in our government and culture. As salt and light in this world, we have a mandate to declare what God's Word says regarding proper conduct. It is imperative that we continue to hold up a standard of righteousness and do what we can to stem the tide of wickedness that constantly crashes against the church and our nation. As is often the case, we need to do the one without neglecting the other.

The design for the family of God is that we come together, expose our sin and struggles, and find the help and encouragement we need to walk in a manner pleasing to the Lord.

But if we walk in the light as He is in the light, we have fellowship with one another, and the blood of Jesus Christ His Son cleanses us from all sin. If we say that we have no sin, we deceive ourselves, and the truth is not in us. If we confess our sins, He is faithful and just to forgive us our sins and to cleanse us from all unrighteousness. (1 John 1:1-9)

In my years as a believer, I've never met anyone claiming to be without sin. But even though none have admitted to being free from sin, it's incredibly rare to talk with someone who feels comfortable admitting which sin they're struggling with.

To walk in the light means you and I are living in such a way that there isn't anything hidden. True fellowship can only happen when we can open the doors of our life and expose ourselves to others. Since there is no one without sin, it shouldn't surprise us to learn the people sitting next to us on Sunday morning have areas in their lives that are less than pretty. Neither should we live under the notion that others expect us to be free from the blemishes of sin.

It is only when we allow the less-than-desirable areas of our life to be brought into the light that the blood of Jesus cleanses us.

Notice 1 John 1:7's wording: "If we walk in the light . . . we have fellowship . . . and the blood of Jesus cleanses us." Then James 5:16's wording: "Confess your trespasses to one another . . . that you may be healed."

In light of Scripture, we see power and freedom, even healing and cleansing that are released into a believer's life through fellowship and confession. It's easy to see why the enemy would work so hard to convince us not to trust one another and not to be open about our sins and struggles. He knows as long as he can convince us to hide our sin and battle against him alone, he has a much better chance of deceiving and controlling us.

Without the support, correction, and encouragement from Christian fellowship, we fight battles we weren't designed to win. As a result, many of us typically do one of two things:

Some will quit, deciding since they can't succeed as a Christian, they might as well live their lives for themselves and the world. Then they re-embrace the very sin, deception, and bondage that Christ freed them from. Before long, they're right back where they were—or worse—before following the Lord.

Others will take on a form of godliness, lacking any real power. That usually involves creating or adopting a subset of rules to live by and focusing on behavior modification to provide a sense of self-righteousness. Unfortunately, it most often involves the compulsion to judge others who aren't measuring up to the guidelines they've created. Instead of comparing themselves to Christ, they compare themselves to others, using those who fall short of their self-imposed standard as proof of their superiority.

There are several reasons why we resist being open about our struggles: We don't want people to think less of us, we are afraid of being rejected, and we don't want to lose credibility as Christians, to name a few.

When we begin to break down the mechanics behind our silence, we find it's rooted in attitudes and emotions that aren't fruits of the Spirit. For example, pride is at the root of our desire to be elevated in the eyes of our peers. Fear of man is at the root of our compulsion to be accepted. Self-righteousness is at the root of our efforts to be *good* Christians. There aren't many godly reasons at the heart of these for not being open and vulnerable with each other.

In Section 3, you'll find practical ways to address this issue on an individual level. At this point, however, I feel compelled to encourage you—if you're struggling with the silence of sin, take heart. I realize it can be extremely frightening to consider someone possibly finding out about your sin. Let me assure you that at the right time and in the right setting, there is no greater freedom than what you'll experience by opening that door.

One of the tactics the enemy uses to keep believers in bondage is to keep them locked up in guilt and shame. He does that because he knows how powerful and liberating it is to have fellowship in Christ. He is terrified because he knows it only takes two believers standing in agreement to release God's kingdom and power.

૮૩૪૦

Pressure to Conform

Another pervasive attitude in the church at large is the idea that it's more important to modify external behavior than it is to pursue spiritual and emotional healing.

The message is communicated, verbally and otherwise: "When you become a Christian, stop doing bad things and start doing good things." As noble and right as this message sounds, it's at the heart of the problem.

I'm not saying we should ignore sin or advocate people continue in sinful behavior after they come to Christ. What I am saying is the most important thing for a new believer to focus on is not the issue of sin. Addressing issues of wrong and right causes us to inadvertently train people to be shallow, self-righteous, and hypocritical. Instead of truly getting free from sin, they are simply being inoculated against the life of the Holy Spirit and learning to depend on the flesh. As believers, we aren't called to the ministry of behavior modification—we're called to the ministry of reconciliation and the mandate of discipleship.

The problem with an environment that encourages silence regarding sin is that it pressures people to look good and acceptable on the outside without ever dealing with the issues of the heart. When we focus on condemning anything that doesn't look *right*, it may make people easier to tolerate, but we make it harder to know the true heart issues they may be struggling with. Since everyone seems to appear *good*, we look around at other believers and think everyone else but me has it all together.

As difficult as it would be to live with, it would be much more beneficial if people didn't hide their sin behind a facade of acceptable behavior. Instead of gestating for months and years only to explode in scandalous proportions, most issues could be handled without the heartache and drama surrounding the *fall* of the believer, not the least of which are ministers.

To be sure, there are times when we need to inform a new believer to "go and sin no more." There were several times those words were the Lord's command to the one He had saved. One was the woman caught in adultery, and the other was the infirmed man by the pool of Bethesda. A much more common call than "go and sin no more" was "come and follow me."

Our call, our commission, is to make disciples. I submit to you that if we did that one thing, we wouldn't need to tell people to stop sinning—they would do that on their own as we imparted the principles and revelations of living by the Spirit.

Sin is not the problem. It can certainly cause problems, but it isn't the problem. The crux of the sin problem isn't sin itself, but the fallen nature of man that needs to be redeemed.

I'm sure you would agree the Christian walk is infinitely more than just trying not to sin. Jesus didn't come so we wouldn't sin. He came to give us life—life more abundantly. When we learn to live the life God has for us and begin to experience the righteousness, peace, and joy in the Holy Spirit, sin will begin to lose its appeal in a hurry.

It is vital that we allow people to be real. If they are struggling with sin, then that's a great indication they need to be trained and discipled. Jesus often referred to the reality of sin as darkness and to His life as light. As we consider the nature of light and darkness, we can see that regardless of how much we point out the darkness, it does nothing to remove it. The spiritual condition of many believers is they're trying to look like candles instead of being vessels of light.

It's been said the world is more aware of what the church is against than what it's for. This same thing can be said of most people who are in the church as well. They know what they aren't supposed to do, but struggle to find victory and purpose beyond that.

In all actuality, sin is nothing more than the symptom of the problem. That is why we will never succeed at affecting change by focusing on sin. Most often, there is a lie, a wound, or an unmet need at the root of sin. To try removing sin from our lives to be *right* with God is the equivalent of picking the apples off an apple tree to get it to become an orange tree. To truly be free from sin, we need to allow Jesus Christ to visit the root of our need and apply the truth of His Word in that area of our heart.

The culture of silence and the pressure to conform in the body of Christ are symptoms. They are symptoms of the greatest problem we face. At the core of these and many other issues is a lack of clarity regarding the full message of the Gospel of Jesus Christ.

෦෫෮

God is Withholding from You

Throughout my life this lie has been a challenge for me. I suspect it may be for you as well.

The truth is God is able to give us everything we need and want, and yet sometimes He chooses not to. He could heal every hurt, and yet He allows us to feel pain instead. He could remove every obstacle, and yet they remain—immovable. He could shield us from failure, yet it's only after we fall flat on our face He reveals to us the folly of our way.

If He can do all these things, why doesn't He? From our perspective, it may seem He is holding out on us.

I remember one day when I was pastoring in California and facing various relational, situational, and financial challenges. I'd wearied myself, doing everything I thought I was supposed to do so God would move. I fasted, prayed, worshipped. I stood in agreement with every declaration from God's Word I could think of. I confessed every sin I could think of and anything I thought I might have overlooked. There was no stone left unturned, and yet the heavens seemed like brass.

One afternoon, I'd finally had it. I looked toward the heavens and shouted, "I'm done. I'm sick and tired of trying to do all this stuff. I'm done. I'm through. I'm never going to be able to measure up to all that you expect of me!"

As clearly as you can imagine, I heard the Lord say, "Finally!"

"What?" I was stunned. "Finally?"

I'd been waiting for the Lord to respond to all of my effort, all my passion, all my self-righteousness. And when I *finally* realized that for all my effort the Lord wouldn't be moved . . . we could begin. At the end of myself, I woke up, at least partially, to the reality it was not by my strength, ability, or effort that caused His will to be realized in my life. It's in Him, with Him, and through Him that I live.

God was withholding something from me, but not in the way I thought. I thought there was something good He was reluctant to give me. In fact, He was withholding these things from me for my own good—to benefit me, to do good and cause good for me.

The truth is God loves to give good gifts to me and to you. It is His pleasure to give us the fullness of His kingdom. He will never withhold anything good from you. There may be a delay. There may be times when what you think is good would actually be harmful to you. There may be times when God has something better than the good thing you want right now. When we know His heart, we can trust the delays and even the denials of our requests. He will not withhold anything good from you. He will make all things beautiful in their time.

We are absolutely assured God is not interested in withholding anything from us. It is His desire to give us every good gift to enjoy. So here's an important question to ask yourself: Am I withholding anything from God?

CRWO

From Information to Application

Most of what has been covered up to this point is a foundation for the next part of the book. Having a solid understanding of the dynamics of wounds and the pain they cause will better equip you to walk through the healing process.

SECTION 3:

FACE YOURSELF

Chapter 15

The Offense

Welcome to the trailhead of the path where the focus turns toward your heart. Everything up to this point prepared you to take these next steps . . . leading to your personal freedom.

The principles, truths, observations, and insights presented on the following pages are submitted as tools. The Healer is the Holy Spirit and you'll need His guidance and direction to navigate through the journey before you.

There may be some things in this chapter that will make you feel like I have a hidden camera following you around. There may be some things that have absolutely nothing to do with your particular situation. Either way, that's okay.

These are guidelines that can help you, but they are not formulas. The steps outlined help direct you to key areas in your heart that are connected to your struggles. I'll include some worksheets, pose some questions, and include some prayers I've brought before the Lord. Feel free to use them.

These types of tools have been helpful as I visited many painful areas in my heart. There's no power in the outlines, questions, or prayers per se, but they may help guide you through the emotions of the moment. Personally, there were times I felt so overwhelmed by the feelings I was processing that it helped me to have an external reference point to navigate the path.

● ● ●

I've used these steps many times—for myself and with others. I've watched as the Lord released breakthrough after breakthrough, and I know He desires to do the same for you. It's my hope that the things I've shared will help you find wholeness and freedom as well.

CKUO

Where to Begin

I was sitting in my office working on a project when I heard Helen cry out from the kitchen.

"Honey, come here! Quickly!"

I knew she'd been out working in the backyard, but I had no idea what was about to greet me when I walked into the kitchen.

"What's going on?"

"Look!" She pointed to a large, sprawling weed lying across the counter—dirt and all.

"Okay . . . " I had no idea why a huge weed was defiling our counter.

Helen said she'd been weeding near the flowers when the Lord drew her attention to this weed. The weed, a spurge, was covering a large portion of the flowerbed. As she examined the weed's branches, she discovered that although there were dozens of branches stretched out on the ground, they all led back to one single root near the center. She began to dig and found that the root was deep. As she pulled it out, the Lord spoke to her and said, "There are many things in your life that you are trying to change, but it isn't by cutting the branches that you'll be free—you need to go to the deep roots from which they grow."

Helen had been asking the Lord to help her deal with anger, jealousy, envy, and a number of other feelings and behaviors that were troubling her. But, as the Lord revealed, it wasn't anger or jealousy or any of the other manifestations she was struggling with—something beneath each of those was springing forth. There was a wound hidden beneath.

Most often we're drawn to try to change the behaviors at the surface. The Lord is concerned with the heart. The best approach is to ask the Lord to reveal the areas keeping you from the abundant life He wants for you. Then let Him direct you from there.

ᎧᎬᏃᎴ

What Happens Next

If you want to purify gold, you need to turn up the heat. There is nothing like difficult people and/or circumstances to bring things to the surface. As you ask the Lord to identify where He wants to start, you can expect events and situations to expose what is hidden. When that happens, remember that you asked the Lord to reveal whatever is hindering you. I know that seems rhetorical, but I was caught off guard when I first started asking Him to expose my wounds. When the circumstances come, stand fast in the knowledge that He is answering you and is helping you. Cooperate with Him.

Challenging situations highlight sensitive areas in your heart. These areas are sensitive for a reason. Your thoughts, attitudes, and actions may contain symptoms, revealing there is more to the situation than meets the eye. In fact, there are a number of ways you already are giving yourself clues regarding which areas of your heart are ready to be healed.

This chapter highlights common places to discover your wounds. As you read through the following paragraphs, make note of the specific details relating to your life. There are several pages at the end of the chapter to record any thoughts, feelings, or situations that stand out to you.

ᎧᎬᏃᎴ

❋ ❋ ❋

What to Look for

Painful Memories

Memories are a natural part of life. Not all memories are pleasant, but regardless of the nature of the memory, it shouldn't cause pain. Pain is an indication there is an unhealed wound.

Physical wounds are extremely sensitive. But once they're healed, you can touch the scar without feeling any pain. It's the same with the soul. An unhealed area in your heart will be sensitive to the touch.

Take note of any painful memories—they will be a part of the healing process. The Lord will visit these memories with His healing power to redeem them.

Off-limit Topics

There are some subjects that families and individuals know not to bring up. In some cases, these are the 500-pound gorillas that everyone knows about, but are afraid or unwilling to discuss. Some are family secrets that are taboo. When the subject is even close to being brought up, it's met with responses like *we don't talk about that*. Other subjects may be personal ones—often painful or shameful—we'd rather forget they ever happened.

When you encounter any of these off-limit subjects that are intentionally avoided, whether covertly or overtly—take note. Most often these topics are laced with thoughts and beliefs that are negatively impacting your day-to-day life.

I would also like to point out that the power of the enemy is greatly exaggerated in the darkness. He thrives on keeping the painful areas in your heart shrouded in shadow because he knows he will lose his power when it is brought into the light.

There have been areas of my past where the enemy exerted guilt, shame, and embarrassment to control, manipulate, and criticize me. The simple act of bringing these things of my past into the light by confessing it to a fellow believer brought about a freedom that was life-changing.

People You Avoid

I don't believe we need to be friends with everyone. In fact, there are some folks we really need to avoid—whether for safety or sanity. And to be completely clear, there are times when I've counseled people to permanently remove themselves from others for a number of reasons, which I'll leave to your imagination.

That being said, there is a healthy process to determine the motives for wanting to avoid someone. The real issue—as it pertains to identifying wounds—isn't about if you should or shouldn't avoid certain people, but why. Is the person truly dangerous or just annoying? Do they remind you of someone else who caused you pain in the past? Are there unresolved issues with the person that you're unable or unwilling to address? These are the kinds of questions that will help identify if the avoidance is really an attempt to circumvent pain or if it's something else.

As you evaluate your relationship with these people, consider how you feel and which emotions are evoked. If you feel anger, go deeper. What's beneath the anger? Is it pain or fear? Is it because there was an unmet need that left you feeling hurt or undervalued?

Physical Pain Associated with an Emotional Response

During a heated argument with my wife, I'd stated my opinions regarding the matter at hand. In her defense, Helen said, "I don't care what you think!" I knew she was reacting to the frustration of the moment, but her words were like a punch to my gut. I literally felt physical pain in my stomach when I heard them.

Any time you have a physical reaction to a situation or statement, it's a good indication you're carrying a wound in that area of your soul. Consider the words that caused a reaction in your physiology (sweating, physical pain, anxiety, dry mouth, etc.). But especially note reactions that cause pain.

Cyclical Patterns

Why does this always happen to me? Why do I always end up in relationships like this? These are actually great conversation-starter questions before the Lord.

Look for cyclical patterns in your life that are typically destructive in nature. Terms like *always* and *never* are good clues that something is afoot.

Sometimes it feels like you're in a rut. You may find yourself having the same basic argument with people over and over. Or you may find that people *always treat you* in a certain way. Or you seem to repeatedly find yourself in relationships with people that all have the same character trait that troubles you.

It could also manifest as repetitive actions or reactions that cause pain in you or others. Addictive behaviors would definitely fall into this category.

Disproportionate Emotional Responses

I was driving on the freeway in California one morning on my way to work. I'd just passed a car in the slow lane and turned on my signal to shift lanes. The light of my blinker must have had quite an impact on the elderly gentleman I had just passed, because he quickly accelerated to close the gap between him and the car ahead of him so I couldn't change lanes. As I looked out of my passenger window, I saw a red-faced, gray-haired gentleman mouthing words that I assumed were not too flattering. In addition, he clearly expressed his displeasure at my attempted lane change with some gestures that left little room for personal interpretation.

Although I can certainly relate to the frustration of driving in commuter traffic, this particular response would fall into a category I'd classify as disproportionate to the stimuli.

I am not judging this individual, because I could have given any number of examples of my own road-rage-ish reactions over the years. In some ways, I would consider his expression to be mild compared to mine. However, it's an example of how our emotions will find a way to the surface.

There are times when we're touched in tender areas of our heart. Our reaction may seem like a correct response since it's proportionate to the pain we feel. For those who don't carry the same wound as we do, our response can be quite confusing. It's even possible that we might look back at our reaction and wonder why it was so intense. That's simply another indication that there is something at the root that may need to be healed.

Pay attention to the dynamics in these various situations. There will always be clues as to what may lie beneath the surface.

Controlling or Unrealistic Fear

Fear is not good or bad in and of itself. It can be good and keep us from dangerous situations. It also has the capacity to be bad if it's rooted in a wound.

For the first ten years of our marriage, Helen had an overwhelming fear of snakes. At first I thought it might have been rooted in her growing up in Brazil—protective warnings from loved ones. There weren't many snakes in the area she'd lived, but she spent a significant amount of time with relatives in more-remote locations. In those areas, there were many deadly snakes.

We began to suspect there might be more to the story since she couldn't even see a picture of a snake in a book, computer, or any display. It would be perfectly natural and healthy to fear going near or picking up a deadly snake, but to be overwhelmed with fear from seeing a picture is unrealistic. There was no danger. No threat. And yet her fear was real.

Helen, two of our children, and I were at a street fair in Manteca, California, one afternoon with some dear friends and their children. Helen and I were browsing at a jewelry craft stand; she was examining some cute, feather earrings. About fifty feet behind her was a young man with a yellow boa constrictor on his shoulders. The thing was about seven or eight feet long. The kids knew about Helen's fear, and I could see they were excited to see her reaction.

I knew this wouldn't turn out well, so I calmly turned to Helen and asked her to look at me. She looked at me and I quietly told her to keep her eyes on me. The kids began calling to her encouraging her to look. "Honey," I said firmly, "just keep looking at me. Don't turn around."

Of course her curiosity got the better of her and she turned. The man and snake were now about twenty feet away.

Everyone on the street turned to see what tragedy had happened as Helen's scream pierced the air. The earrings she had been examining went flying through the air as Helen ran so fast all we could see was a blur. I have to admit that the blur may have been because my eyes were watering from laughing so hard. Once the laughter died down and the snake and his carrier had cleared the area, Helen returned to the jewelry stand to apologize and buy a slightly worn pair of earrings.

The snake incident was funny to a degree—well, for everyone except Helen—but it really was an indication that something in her heart needed attention. In this case, she'd adopted the fearful response from an older relative's reaction to snakes. Although there was never any real danger at the street fair, Helen's trauma was real, rooted in her relative's fear and intense emotional reaction to snakes.

Many of the fears that control people are anything but fun. They are rooted in painful—and often traumatic—circumstances, entrapping us in prisons of fear. The following poem is something I wrote as the Lord was revealing the nature of fear and self-preservation in me.

Walls

Walls
They protect me
They keep me from harm

Walls
They imprison me
They keep me from help

Walls
They comfort me
They keep me from hate

Walls
They isolate me
They keep me from love

I wrote this shortly after the year 2000. In the aftermath of my life's turmoil, I discovered I was afraid to connect with people. Afraid to be vulnerable. Afraid of rejection. I realized how the walls I was building around my life could keep people out, but at the expense of my freedom.

Look for areas in your life where fear may be at work. Look at what you're afraid of and what steps you've taken to protect yourself from realizing your fears.

Self-preservation

Closely tied with fear is the desire for self-preservation. Once again, I'm not talking about a healthy separation from yourself and something dangerous.

Unhealthy or unbalanced self-preservation is usually associated with an unwillingness to be hurt, be vulnerable, or to trust.

As followers of Jesus Christ, there will always be a certain level of vulnerability and sacrifice associated with our walk. That is the example He gave and the one He has invited us to follow. This type of sacrifice is out of obedience to the leading of the Holy Spirit and will be for a redemptive purpose.

This doesn't suggest that the Lord is asking you to remain in abusive and destructive relationships or to subject yourself to circumstances that are emotionally, spiritually, physically, or psychologically damaging.

Betty was a middle-aged Christian woman, married to a verbally/physically abusive, alcoholic man. Frequently, she'd be seen with bruises on her face and arms. Betty wanted to be a good Christian woman and submit to her husband, but she didn't know how much more she could take.

She scheduled a meeting with her pastor, who counseled her to keep praying and submit to her husband. After all, divorce was a sin and God didn't want her to sin. She returned home only to be hospitalized due to the severity of the beating. Thankfully the law intervened and she was liberated from the abuse.

Let me be perfectly clear. Under no circumstance would I encourage someone to return to an abusive situation like that. I would recommend that any pastor or counselor who feels a person should stay in a situation like that volunteer to take that person's place. If you're convinced it is the right thing to do, then it's only right that you bear the same burden you expect your brother or sister to bear.

I bring Betty's situation to the forefront to clearly state that it would be a natural and healthy response to preserve yourself from that situation.

On the other side of the spectrum, if you're building walls around yourself and trying to prevent yourself from having relationships because you might get hurt, that's another story. If you've come out of an abusive situation, you will need healing and restoration, but not *self*-preservation. If you're protecting and preserving yourself, you may have made an idol out of your own ability to protect.

෴

Recording What Comes to Mind

Painful Memories
What memories cause pain or evoke sorrow, regret, or other types of pain?

Off-limit Topics
What topics do you (or those in your relationships) avoid? Include any thoughts of why you believe that is the case.

People You Avoid
Identify the people you avoid and note any details of why you avoid them. Is it because of past or current issues? Is it because you're uncomfortable around them or do they remind you of someone who makes you feel uncomfortable?

Physical Pain Associated with Emotions
Do you experience painful responses to emotional situations? Describe the situations, emotions, and details of the pain. What type of pain is it and where is it located?

Cyclical Patterns
Do you find yourself in the same type of relationships or situations? Do you feel that certain outcomes are predictable in your life? Describe them here. Consider the situations where you use terms like always or never.

Disproportionate Emotional Responses

Are there times where you find yourself reacting in ways that exceed what others deem appropriate? Describe the dynamics of those situations here. Are there common themes either in your response or in whatever is provoking your response?

Controlling Behavior or Unrealistic Fears

Do you feel insecure, frightened, or angry with certain people or in certain situations if you aren't in control? Do you have unrealistic fears or phobias causing you to avoid people or things?

Areas of Self-preservation

Describe any areas where you go out of your way to protect yourself. Are there certain people or situations you intentionally avoid to protect yourself from being hurt or taken advantage of?

CRBO

Navigating the Discovery Process

Okay, so now you're starting to tap in to some ugliness. This is good. The first part of addressing a wound is to deal with the infection. It's not meant to be pretty—you need to get it out. The reality is that the Lord orders your steps. He is actually orchestrating the events and circumstances in your life to bring certain things out into the light. Here's what you can do when the Lord starts to expose them.

Limit Personal Interactions

When you're feeling triggered by your interaction with a person, do your best to conclude your interaction or excuse yourself from the situation. This isn't to avoid the person or situation, but is your opportunity to stay connected to the thoughts, feelings, and emotions associated with the event. Once you have disengaged, get to a quiet place.

Communicate and Capture

Bring all the hurt and internal dialogue to the Lord. Take notes if that helps. Regardless of what it takes to get to the root, once you're connected to it, ask the Lord to shine His light and help you identify the thoughts, ideas, and beliefs associated with it. You're believing something—and that something is not true. If it was true, it would be producing peace and joy within you.

Welcome the Lord into the Mess

Invite the Holy Spirit into what He is revealing and thank Him for exposing it so you can be healed and set free from it. Remind yourself of God's promises and the fact that God loves you, is committed to you, and that this is a process of deliverance. This might sound overly simplistic right now, but believe me, you'll need it.

Investigate

As the Lord reveals the *what*, ask Him about the *why*.

These four tools will help you discover hidden wounds, but there is a real possibility that you already know where some of your struggles come from. Whether or not you need help finding them, once you do, then what? You need to clearly define the offense.

ভশ

Chapter 16

Stage 1: The Heart of the Offense

Discovering the wounded areas of your heart is just the starting point. The next step is examining the source of that pain to understand its true impact.

This part is going to be unique to you. I've worked through this process with many people and each person has been different. There are some things you can do to help sort through the process.

Like the other phases, the first step is to ask the Holy Spirit to help you. He'll absolutely guide you to where you need to go. Everything I am sharing in this book is the result of asking Him for help—He helped me and He will help you.

When you identify the wounds in your heart, try to remember the first time you felt that pain. Consider the impact of that event:

- What did you believe about yourself?
- What did you conclude about others?
- What decisions did you make in your heart?
- What promises or vows did you make to yourself?
- What things did you determine you'd never do?

- What things did you commit yourself to doing with your life?

Invite the Holy Spirit into your woundedness and pain. There is a worksheet available in the appendix of this book to help you with this step. Here are some things to keep in mind:

- Be honest, transparent. (Just to let you in on a secret—He already knows!) Be real.
- Thank the Lord for His faithfulness and kindness to reveal these things—remind yourself that the only reason He does that is so you can be healed and set free for the abundant life He purchased for you.
- Pray. "Lord, (this emotion/pain) is what I'm feeling. I ask you to come into this part of my life to heal and restore me. Help me see this event from your perspective."

As uncomfortable as it may be, it's important to spend some time digging into and understanding the offense you've identified. The following steps will help bring clarity to the scope of each wound and the influence it has had on your life.

Acknowledge the Offense
An important part of this journey is to attempt to fully understand the implications of what happened. Just as it would be vitally important to thoroughly examine a physical wound, so it is with the wound of your heart. To move forward, you must simply and clearly acknowledge that you've been hurt and that an offense has taken place.

Consider the Impact

The things that were done or said to you, or the things you were wrongfully exposed to, caused damage. They hurt you and distorted your view of the world and the people in it. It distorted your view of God and of yourself—and that caused a chain reaction of pain and hardship in your life. It has made it virtually impossible for you to have a normal healthy life. It has impeded your ability to connect with others. It has robbed you of your innocence. Violated your trust. Ravaged your identity. A ripple effect has extended out from this place of pain and caused damage to you and others.

Honesty. That's the answer to the question I can almost hear you asking, "Why is He stirring this up? This isn't helping . . . it's making me mad!" Yes, honesty. We have been lied to and we even lied to ourselves to try to mentally minimize the impact of what we've been through.

To really walk this through, you'll need an honest assessment of the damage and grasp its repercussions. That's for several reasons. One is so you can measure the impact of the healing. The other is to prepare for something you're going to need to do that is usually one of the most difficult steps for most of the people I work with: forgive.

Don't worry if you aren't sure if you're ready to forgive. We'll address that whole thing shortly.

As you dig into the realities of how the offense has impacted you, you'll see beliefs, ideas, attitudes, and actions that have come as a result—perhaps even the feelings and behaviors that were your clues to get to the root of the wound.

Judge the Behavior

The thing that was done to you was wrong. Whether well-intentioned or evil. Whether intentional or accidental. It wasn't right.

I'm not asking you to judge the person—we'll discuss what to do with the person later. I'm asking you to judge the behavior.

Abusive behavior is wrong. You may have been told you deserved it or it was your fault, but I assure you, it isn't true. You didn't deserve it and it wasn't your fault. I'll say that again: You didn't deserve that. It wasn't your fault. I promise you.

The inappropriate sexual exposure you had was not your fault. You didn't do anything to cause that. There is no justification and no excuse for how you were treated. What was done to you was wrong.

The words spoken to you and about you were hurtful and they were wrong. There was nothing wrong with you. You didn't deserve to be called those names. You were not—nor are you—stupid, lazy, ugly. You are not an accident and you are wanted. To tell you anything else was wrong and you didn't deserve that.

Avoid any temptation to excuse or justify the behavior against you. Since it's often the case that our wounds were caused by people we love dearly, we can feel compelled to minimize or explain away the behavior. Remember, we're judging behavior, not people. And remember that our goal is honesty.

The truth is that no matter how you feel about the person that caused this pain, it belongs to you now.

Take Ownership of Your Wound

Blame, anger, bitterness—they do nothing to help you find freedom. No matter who may have been at fault, there is one thing for sure, it happened to you. Now is the time to accept the reality that regardless of the circumstances it's *your* mess now.

What if someone broke into your house in the middle of the night and dumped a trash can full of rotten garbage in your living room? What would you do? You didn't deserve it. It wasn't fair. It wasn't your fault. But there it is. Now you have a choice: Will you clean it up or will you leave it there?

It's your house and it's your decision. Regardless of the mess someone dumped into your life, you'll need to decide if you will do what it takes to clean and restore your home or allow the work of a vandal to determine the condition of your living room.

You could leave it there to fester and ripen, learning how to live around it. You could spend all your time hating and blaming the wretches that poured it into your house. You could invite people over to show them how badly you were treated and gain sympathy. I would not recommend any course of action—or inaction—that would allow this garbage to stay in your life one more second.

Since you have the choice to leave the garbage there, let's see what will happen if you do that:

- It will smell up your life—your home, marriage, job, ministry, etc.
- It's going to get on your children and loved ones
- You will track it everywhere you go—eventually adding to it and dumping some of it into someone else's living room

Any wound you refuse to address in your life will become the same wound in someone else's.

Out of the abundance of the heart the mouth speaks. Regardless of how skilled you may think you are at covering your garbage, it will permeate everything you do to one degree or another.

Something I consider as I sift through the garbage in my own life is the fact that more than likely the person who dumped it in my life had it dumped in their life at some point. This reality in no way justifies or excuses the behavior, but it may give me insight and compassion for my offender.

Let me also say, you may be among the many who have had people you loved and trusted dump some disgusting garbage into your life. You may be carrying deep wounds from your father, mother, spouse, or other family members.

I believe the Lord wants your heart to hear: "It's not your fault." I hear Him say it again with compassion, "Loved one, it's not your fault."

Now that you have spent time digging and clearly identifying an offense that the Lord wants to address, you're ready for Stage 2—your response to what you're seeing.

CRSO

Chapter 17

Stage 2: Your Response

Every destination worthy of a journey has challenges. Some are more difficult than others. Your response to what you've learned up to this point has the power to determine the trajectory of your life. Muster all the tools and information covered so far . . . this is what you've been preparing for.

Getting to the heart of the pain in your soul is a critical step, initiating the healing process. Of equal importance is how you respond to that pain. The way you process the information that's been exposed will determine whether or not healing can begin.

Up to this point, you've taken steps to remove the bandages and expose the wound. You've taken a step back from efforts to mask or dismiss the pain, performing an honest assessment of the damage. Now it is time for debridement. You'll need to remove the dead tissue and clean the wound of the debris and infection that has developed over the years—including removing the damaged, nonviable tissue surrounding the wound so it can begin to heal.

This stage of the journey can be one of the most difficult. It's time to forgive.

Forgive

Once you've clearly identified the offense and its impact in your life, you're ready to walk through the act of forgiving the offender.

Forgiveness is such an important part of the healing journey. In recent years, that has been proven outside of Christian circles in both the secular and medical arenas. Extensive studies with irrefutable results have validated the importance of obeying what the Lord commanded us to do thousands of years ago.

Forgiveness, like the other things the Lord commands us to do, are for our health, healing, wholeness, and safety. These aren't arbitrary rules; they're given for our benefit and our understanding. Coming to a greater place of understanding is the goal at this stage of the process.

Simply put, forgiveness is the act of relinquishing the requirement of being repaid.

In the process of forgiveness, you give up your right for restitution and entrust the process of justice to a loving and gracious God who will deal rightly with the offender. As far as it remains with you, the offender will owe you nothing.

Consider this parable: My wife borrowed $10,000 from my father with no ability to repay the debt. As time progressed, the awkwardness of the debt and her inability to pay caused her to withdraw from the relationship with my dad. Because of my desire to see the relationship restored, I sold all the resources I had and paid the debt.

Now, let me ask a question. At any time after that point, would it be right for my father to ask my wife for more money? When you and I forgive those who have sinned against us, we are in fact acknowledging the price for their sin has already been paid. Jesus Christ took the sin of our offenders at the same time he took ours.

All of us, without exception, owed a debt that we couldn't pay. To hold another person in debt to us is to reject the provision of Jesus Christ's death on the cross.

In a very real and literal way, Jesus took the offense that was done to you and put it on Himself. If you feel you have the right or the need for restitution, go to Jesus to demand payment. Since He is the one now carrying this offense, will you forgive Him?

Without question, the most prevalent obstacle I've encountered in the people I've counseled has been unforgiveness. Partly because of a misunderstanding regarding what forgiveness is (and isn't)—and partly because of a real need we all have in our hearts for justice.

Unforgiveness is Sin

Early in my life I was tormented by the memories of hurtful events that had taken place in my life. I tried and tried to forgive and forget, but the memories, the pain, and the rage continued to swell in my heart and mind. I tried numerous religious methods for forgiving—imagining the offender as a bird in a cage and letting it fly free, writing the offender a letter and burning it, etc. But nothing brought me peace.

As I cried out to the Lord, He brought me to the passage in Matthew 18:21-35, where Jesus explains the importance of forgiveness and the consequence of not giving it. I realized that I, like the wicked servant in the story, was unwilling to truly forgive even after I'd been forgiven of all my sin. The Lord clearly showed me that my judgment and unforgiveness were sin. Then He brought me to 1 John 1:9 and assured me that if I would confess my sin, He would forgive me and cleanse me.

I scheduled an appointment with a godly man I knew and asked if he would be a witness as I confessed my sin of unforgiveness. He agreed. We invited the Holy Spirit to expose every area and instance where I was holding on to that sin, and then I opened the floodgates. For about two hours, I agreed with the Lord about every instance of anger, hate, and unforgiveness He brought to my mind. I acknowledged it was sin and received His forgiveness and cleansing of all my unrighteousness.

I don't know what the person thought of me, but it didn't matter. All I know is that I've never been the same since. I was truly free. I literally felt like a hundred pounds had been lifted off me. In that place where I'd known only hate and rage, I was completely at peace.

If you're holding on to the hurt, pains, and injustices of the past (or present), agree with the Lord that it's sin. As you confess it to Him, you can accept His forgiveness and righteousness by agreeing with the truth.

An Act of the Will

Since forgiveness is a commandment, you're able to do it. The Lord never requires something of us that He won't give the corresponding ability to act upon.

I am not suggesting it's easy, but it is doable. One of the reasons people feel it is impossible is because they are waiting until they *feel* like forgiving. That is a rarity. The great news is you don't have to feel like it to do it. Forgiveness is a choice you make to obey the Father. It's an act of the will that says . . .

"Father, in obedience to you, I choose to forgive this person. I relinquish any rights or debts I previously held and consider this person forgiven before you. I trust you to deal with them according to your loving-kindness, the same way I desire you to deal with me."

You don't need to feel like it. You don't need to like it. You just need to trust the Lord enough to obey Him.

In all honesty, I confess to you that I have forgiven many people, not because I wanted to. It wasn't for their sake—it was for mine. **The willingness to relinquish my self-centered, distorted view of justice is a small price to pay for the freedom I've received through my obedience to forgive.**

● ● ●

The more I've learned about God's love and kindness toward me, the easier it has become to forgive others for the perceived offenses they've done against me. I've also learned the beauty and power of my prayers—not just to forgive, but bless those who've wronged me.

Forgiveness Isn't Saying What Happened is Okay

Sin is sin whether it is committed by us or against us. And sin is never okay. When someone sins against me, and subsequently apologizes, I never say that it's okay. I will forgive them if needed, but I'll never condone a course of action that is outside of what conforms to Christ. In some cases, I believe the best thing we can do for ourselves and for people perpetrating destructive behaviors is to separate ourselves from the situation or individual. Temporarily or permanently, if appropriate. But under no circumstance do I excuse sinful behavior.

Pain in the Process of Forgiveness

Forgiveness is the first crucial part of the healing process, but it's only one part. Working through the complexities of healing is a separate process. Many people have short-circuited the healing process because they thought that once they forgave the person, they shouldn't think about the event any longer.

If you're feeling pain, allow yourself the freedom to express your emotions. Emotions are neither good, nor bad. They are simply a reflection of your current state. God has given us emotions for good reason, so you're not required to deny them. Remember to invite the Holy Spirit into your emotions, whatever they may be. God is not put off or intimidated by your expressions of anger, sadness, or sorrow.

There were times my counselor encouraged me to express my emotions during our session, using whatever verbiage seemed to fit best, regardless of whether or not it was socially acceptable. At the time, the emotional intensity for what I was feeling couldn't be adequately expressed with anything other than a string of curse words that could curl your hair.

Decorum is much less important than the freedom to use whatever language necessary in the cathartic process of expressing your emotions. Expressing your emotions from the depth of your heart will bring much more healing than pretending it isn't there or trying to medicate or suppress it.

Pain is a gift—a mechanism to recognize that something needs attention. It's not a measurement of right and wrong or of your righteousness. If you're feeling pain, it's time to ask the Holy Spirit to show you the source of that pain and to identify the wound. It's not evidence you're doing something wrong.

If you obey the Lord and forgive the person who wounded you, but still feel pain, give yourself permission to walk through the emotional healing process without allowing guilt to make you think you haven't forgiven them.

Forgiveness Doesn't Always Heal the Wound

There may be times when the act of forgiving will bring healing, but that doesn't make it the same process. There are two things happening—sometimes simultaneously. But at other times, the two may be completely independent of one another.

Imagine you and I are hanging out together, and I decide to stab you in the back with a knife. You reel from the pain and I start to feel really bad about it. I decide what I did was wrong, then apologize and ask you to forgive me. Because of your love for the Lord and kindness of your heart, you decide to forgive me. Will that stop your pain?

I am free and clear, but you still have a real issue. A real wound. Just because you forgave me doesn't undo the damage I caused you. It doesn't remove the knife from your back. And it doesn't stop the bleeding or magically remove the danger of infection.

To be absolutely sure, forgiveness is one of the steps you must take in the early stages of healing. Without it, you won't be able to fully recover. But to suggest it's the only step is naive and can even be dangerous.

It is dangerous for several reasons. Forgiveness does nothing to remove the original offense or address the subsequent damage. In addition, it opens up a wide door of guilt, shame, and accusation from the enemy. Instead of seeing the pain you're feeling as a natural result and indication of something that is damaged, you feel condemned that you're still feeling pain. So instead of inviting the Lord into the pain to help you walk through it, you deny the wound and step onto a perpetual cycle of condemnation, asking God to forgive you for your unforgiveness while *trying to forgive* the offender over and over again.

Forgiveness is an act of your will. It can affect your feelings, but has nothing to do with your feelings. You can still feel pain after you forgive, just as you can hold on to unforgiveness without feeling bad about it one bit.

Let me also encourage you to give yourself the freedom to navigate through these issues without an expectation of what you should or shouldn't feel. It's not about answering all the questions and coming up with a formulaic method with theological underpinnings. The important issue is that you're walking through a much-needed healing process with the Lord to bring you into the full measure of healing and wholeness available to you in Christ.

Forgive and Remember

In addition to the previous paradigm, the idea you need to forget about the events of your past is foolish. God has given you the capacity to remember for a reason. The process of healing you're going through requires you to revisit painful areas of your past—including offenses, abuse, mistreatment, trauma, etc. Areas some people would suggest you forget.

In reality, you aren't able to *forget* about the past. You may mask it, bury it, deny it, or ignore it, but you can't forget it. My goal with this book is to help you allow the Lord to heal that memory so it won't cause pain and difficulty when you do remember it. That memory will be transformed from a painful reminder of your past to a testimony and a source of encouragement to share with others.

As shared previously, an open wound turns to a scar that can be touched without pain. So too will your wounds be healed. And in time, you'll be able to touch them and talk about them without pain.

The true test that a wound has been healed is not measured by your inability to recollect it, but by your ability to recount the events without pain.

Layers

Don't be surprised if the Lord revisits the same or similar offenses with you. You may often find layers of damage or even separate wounds associated with the same offense.

Billy was thirteen years old when his father moved out of the house and got his own apartment. His parents had been arguing with raised voices more and more frequently—some of those arguments mentioned Billy's name. He felt his behavior had somehow contributed to their separation. One day Billy was visiting his dad and apologized for not being a good son. He promised his dad that if he would just come home, he'd try to be better. His dad remained silent.

Billy wasn't the problem between his parents. He wasn't even part of the problem. His dad had a responsibility in that moment to communicate that fact with Billy, as well as assure him that he had done nothing wrong and there was nothing wrong with him. There was a real need in Billy's heart to hear those words. Since his father didn't, Billy came up with his own conclusions.

When we first walked through the healing process, he had identified the wound his father caused through a burden of blame and the fear of not being good enough or worthy to be approved and accepted. At a later time, the Lord touched again on this same event as part of Billy's journey to destroy the fear of abandonment. Even though it was a single event, there were multiple offenses and several healing journeys. If we had held to the notion that the event was now somehow off limits, we would have missed this other vital point of restoration.

Confess Your Sin

To confess is simply to agree with God. When I find that my behavior, past or present, is inconsistent with my identity in Christ, I simply agree with God regarding how He views my actions.

I've found that having trustworthy people in my life is incredibly valuable when it comes to confession. Not that I need to confess my sins to someone from a sense of religious duties. No, this is a relational decision to open myself up to the body of Christ around me. There have been some topics that were limited to my wife and counselor, some to close friends, and many other topics that I've talked about publicly. As far as I can recall, there is nothing in my life that I have not already confessed and discussed with someone else.

This is the message we have heard from Him and announce to you, that God is Light, and in Him there is no darkness at all. If we say that we have fellowship with Him and yet walk in the darkness, we lie and do not practice the truth; but if we walk in the Light as He Himself is in the Light, we have fellowship with one another, and the blood of Jesus His Son cleanses us from all sin. If we say that we have no sin, we are deceiving ourselves and the truth is not in us. If we confess our sins, He is faithful and righteous to forgive us our sins and to cleanse us from all unrighteousness. If we say that we have not sinned, we make Him a liar and His Word is not in us. (1 John 1:5-10)

This passage depicts the characteristics of a transparent life. Through honest and vulnerable fellowship, you and I will admit our sins, struggles, and shortcomings to one another. When we do, a supernatural cleansing is released in our soul.

Receive Your Forgiveness

I often hear people asking God to forgive them when they do something outside of what they believe God expects of them. It can be part of addressing sinful behavior, but there are a few things that seem out of place once we understand what was accomplished on the cross.

One thing I've observed is a posture of petitioning when some people ask for forgiveness. The emotional conveyance is that there is a level of uncertainty as to whether or not the Lord is going to grant the request. You don't need to approach the Lord like that. He has already paid the price for your forgiveness and has eternally displayed His uttermost desire to grant forgiveness to you without restriction.

Another emotional dynamic I've seen is the saturation of guilt and condemnation that permeates the request before the Lord. To carry guilt, shame, and unworthiness is denying the work of the cross. Those things—that is, our sins—were nailed to the tree and aren't attributed to us. There may be conviction whereby the gravity of our behavior is realized, causing a brokenness. But the Word is clear, there is no condemnation to those who are in Christ Jesus and are walking by the Spirit.

So know that when the Spirit raises your awareness that something is inconsistent with His working in your life, you can go boldly before His throne with the full assurance of faith that He has already removed the eternal penalty of your sin and fully embraces you as a son or daughter. You may feel compelled to apologize, ask forgiveness, or simply agree with Him in what He has pointed to, but you'll never, ever need to grovel, feel shame, or wonder at His willingness to forgive and cleanse us.

● ● ●

Once you have brought the behavior, attitude, or belief to Him, you can immediately receive forgiveness.

If we confess our sins, He is faithful and righteous to forgive us our sins and to cleanse us from all unrighteousness. (1 John 1:9)

This passage is quite clear that if we confess our sin (that's our part), He is faithful and just to forgive us and cleanse us of all unrighteousness (that's His part). By faith, we simply believe and receive our forgiveness and cleansing, which is our righteousness.

Receive Your Righteousness

In the same way you receive forgiveness by faith, so too you receive righteousness.

Contrary to the religious pressure that many of us have experienced in the institutional church, your righteousness is not earned by your behavior—not by what you do, neither by what you don't do.

Your right standing was accomplished for you apart from your effort or input. In fact, there is nothing you can or could ever do to make you righteous. There is no list of behaviors you could avoid that would ever be attributed in the slightest measure to your standing before the Father. There is only one thing you can do. You can choose to receive your righteousness by faith.

In all honesty, do you really think that on any level you can attempt something on your own that could result in your righteousness? Let me completely discourage you from even trying—the truth is that your best efforts are utterly disgusting to the Lord.

For all of us have become like one who is unclean, And all our righteous deeds are like a filthy garment; And all of us wither like a leaf, And our iniquities, like the wind, take us away. (Isaiah 64:6)

As it is written, "There is none righteous, not even one; There is none who understands, There is none who seeks for God; All have turned aside, together they have become useless; There is none who does good, There is not even one." (Romans 3:10-12)

Since there is nothing you and I can do to earn it, our task is clear—receive it by faith. If God declares we are righteous, and He does, then who are we to disregard or disagree with Him?

In the next stage of the journey, you'll address the thoughts and beliefs that have surrounded your interpretation of the events and circumstances of your past.

ഗ്ഞ

Chapter 18

Stage 3: Your Beliefs

Your beliefs determine how you interact with the world around you. Get ready to examine the thoughts, ideas, and conclusions you've made amidst the pain—because you're about to identify the lies and destroy them with the truth.

As you walk through the wounds of the past, it's important to examine the conclusions and beliefs that you adopted as a result of those wounds. I classify those resulting thought patterns as lies because that's exactly what they are.

Identify the Lies

Let's be perfectly clear about another thing—you and I have been deceived. To some degree we are still lacking the full revelation of truth in our lives. It's bothersome to be sure, but the reality is that if we were walking in the full measure of truth, we would be living in the same stature that Jesus Christ walked when He was on the earth.

Since you and I haven't yet arrived at that level, let's accept that we've been holding on to some lies. Once we acknowledge that, we can move to the next step, which is to work with the Holy Spirit to identify those lies. To walk in freedom, the lies must be uncovered—lies about who you are and lies about who the Lord is. These are the two main areas where the enemy unleashes his attacks every chance he gets.

To unpack the wound and the offense, ask the question, "What beliefs about God or myself resulted from what I went through?" And consider questions like these:

- How did I feel about myself as a result of what happened?
- How did that event affect the perception of my value as a son/daughter, man/woman, etc.?
- What statements did I make about myself? (i.e. I'm so stupid. No one really cares about me. I'm not important. Nobody cares about my feelings.)
- Were there feelings of guilt, shame, or embarrassment? If so, what did that tell me about who I am?
- What conclusions did I make about God? Where was He? Why did He allow that to happen?
- How did that event shape my understanding of the Lord?

Once you clarify the lies associated with the event, the next step is to confront them head on.

Break Agreement with the Lies

There is a powerful principle in the Kingdom of God that relates to agreement. Jesus asked the question, "How can two walk together unless they agree?"

Within your belief system, you've been walking in agreement with the lies the enemy has told you. Those lies have led you down paths that have caused pain and sorrow, and perpetuated the wound you had sustained. Those lies are designed to guide you down a path of self-destruction—and up to this point, you've been agreeable. Now it's time to confront and break that agreement.

It is important to call attention to how the enemy works against you. The truth is, he has no power over you—no power except what you give him. When you accept and agree with the lie he offers, it isn't his power, it's your belief in his power that rules. **If you break that agreement, he loses the power to influence you.**

As you identify a lie, use this statement or one similar to verbally break your agreement with it:

"I reject the lie that _____. I break all agreement with this lie and confess my previous agreement as sin. I receive my forgiveness and my righteousness.

Renouncing Guilt and Shame

The first Sunday following my arrest for the incident with Helen, I entered the church alone—the church she and I attended. My behavior toward my wife was one of the worst things I'd done and my head immediately, instinctively, fell in shame as I walked toward my seat. I had only walked a few steps when I heard the Lord speak to me clearly and emphatically. He said, "Don't you ever hang your head in the presence of men, for not one man is worthy to hold his head up before me."

From that day until this, I have never allowed shame or guilt to influence me. Jesus Christ took our guilt and shame upon Himself and it was nailed to the cross with all of our sin. The full penalty for sin was paid. There is nothing else required of us except to receive by faith His provision.

I have pondered many times the Lord's word to me on that day. It is a truth that has become the great equalizer. Just as no one is worthy to hold his head up before the Lord, neither do we have the right to judge another as unworthy of His forgiveness. We are all 100% dependent upon His love, grace, and mercy—without exception. There is none righteous, not even one.

Since that's the case, we are free from shame and free from guilt when it comes to our relationship with the Lord. We renounce all guilt and shame, receiving our forgiveness and our righteousness from Him by faith.

Identify the Truth

Every lie is an attempt to keep you away from the power of Jesus Christ in your life. Our firm assurance is that when we know and abide in the truth, we will walk in freedom.

As you identify the lie, it is intuitive that the truth is the opposite. If the lie is that you are worthless and nobody loves you, then what is the truth? You are loved and greatly valued. If the lie states you are stupid and can't do anything right, what is the truth? You are intelligent and can do all things through Christ who strengthens you.

In most cases, there are specific scriptures that declare who and what God says about you. I encourage you to write those truths down.

Agree with the Truth

The next step is to verbally declare your agreement with the truth of what God says about you. The powerful principle of agreement works with the lie or the truth. When you are in agreement with the truth, it will lead and guide you to life.

Declare Your Agreement

Father, I agree with your truth that I am _____. I thank you that your Word is true and it is impossible for you to lie. Therefore, I stand in agreement with your Word and bind myself together with who you say that I am.

Along with recognizing the lies and replacing them with the truth, you will need to shift the focus of what your heart depends upon. In the past, you've looked to sources other than the One who can actually provide what you need. Now your eyes must look to Him.

CRED

• • •

Chapter 19

Stage 4: Your Source

Where you're going, you'll need to know who and what you can depend on. Placing your hope, trust, or comfort in the wrong person or things can cost you dearly. This is the part of the healing journey where you'll plant your feet on the foundation that won't be shaken.

Along with the lies and distortions associated with our wounds, there is another common area needing to be addressed—how we learned to cope with ourselves under the weight of our pain. As we discussed previously, an idol is anything we look to for what only God can truly supply. Through dismantling lies, you'll begin to see more clearly the structures and methods developed that are rooted in idolatry.

The following narrative is part of my story. You'll see how I had erected idols in my life that had no capacity to give me what I needed.

CʒꞂꝊ

Julie

My knees gave way—my world was crashing around me. Blood poured from my nose as my body slumped to the ground. The blood mixed with tears and ran down my face and clothes. I was aware of little else. The searing agony of my hopes and dreams being violently ripped from me changed my life forever.

I'd met Julie on a warm summer evening, shortly after graduating from high school. The girl of my dreams had stepped into my life and brought joy and hope into the dreary times of my youth. Somehow I knew she was the one I'd spend the rest of my life with. The more time we spent together, the surer I became that the Lord had brought her into my life—the answer to my prayers.

We spent many hours talking and dreaming and planning for our future. Marriage, for sure. Children, a given. Houses, jobs, travel—we'd talked about it all. I loved her and she loved me. There was no doubt in our minds. We were meant to be together.

She lived about an hour and a half away with her parents, working hard to finish the educational requirements of her Christian school so she could graduate early. I also was working hard and pressing in to God, wanting to become the man and future husband He wanted me to be. I'd never been so happy in all my life.

I'd spent a good part of a day in jewelry stores looking for the perfect ring for the perfect girl. But I was a young man without a lot of extra money. Standing before the sparkling merchandise, it didn't take long to realize I needed to approach this whole ring thing in phases.

As I persevered, I found the perfect solution. The plan was foolproof. I pictured it all in my mind and knew I'd rack up a lot of points from Julie— and her family—through my well-conceived, romantic plan.

I'd chosen a Black Hills Gold ring. It was pretty, but not too glamorous. In other words, it fit my limited budget. I decided to wrap it in an oversized box, inside another box, and give it to her for Christmas, which was less than two weeks away. We'd planned to spend the holiday at her parents'.

I'd imagined her opening that first box, then the second. She'd probably start to suspect what it was when she got to the actual ring box, so

I'd planned to quickly drop to my knees in front of her—pledging my heart and life to her right then. I could picture her smiling through tears of joy and my hugging her. Our future would be so happy.

But later that night after buying the ring, I went to my church's midweek prayer service. We'd just begun to pray when my buddy's girlfriend entered the sanctuary crying. My friend excused himself and they headed to the foyer. I continued to pray. Then he came back to the sanctuary and went to his sister; the two of them headed to the foyer. I continued to pray. Then his sister came back to the sanctuary and got the pastor. Again, I continued to pray, but began wondering why there were fewer and fewer people praying.

Eventually I recognized a pattern developing—everyone but me was being invited out of the sanctuary. Then my friend came and sat in the pew behind mine. I was on my knees looking over the back of the pew into his blank face. He shook his head from side to side. I asked what was going on, but the only thing he could say was he didn't know what to say.

At first, I thought something might have happened to one of my family members and he just didn't know how to tell me. I got up and walked into the foyer. Amazingly, the dull clamor of many people talking over each other immediately stopped as they saw me step through the doors. All eyes were on me.

My heart raced and the terrifying reality that something horrible had happened gripped me. This was somehow about me. With each step, I knew my life was about to change and would never be the same.

"Pastor, what's going on?" My tone was clear—avoiding me was no longer an option. He put his arm on my right shoulder as the associate pastor came alongside my left.

"Well, son," he said as the three of us walked out of the church, "I don't know how much of a backbone you have . . . "

"Just tell me."

He sighed and paused, obviously unsure of how to say what needed to be said. We walked quietly into the clear, cold, moonless night. I recall looking up at how brilliantly the stars covered the sky.

Then the pastor drew a quick breath, followed by a brief pause. I braced myself.

"Earlier today your girlfriend killed herself."

Before the words were completely out of his mouth, my body went limp and I collapsed to the ground. Blood oozed from my nose as tears overcame me. Never before, nor since, has such confusion, agony, and grief converged upon me.

To this day I don't know what drove Julie to put a .22-caliber pistol to her head and pull the trigger. It's impossible to articulate the tragedy that took place in my heart, mind, and soul. Loss, despair, anguish, pain—those words are hollow specters of what I felt and how that single event impacted me.

CRBO

Where I Found Comfort

I'd been exposed to drug and alcohol abuse at an early age. Substance abuse had become a source of relief, fun, and forgetfulness for my childhood pain. After Julie's death, I turned to alcohol and promiscuity as my primary comfort sources.

During the following months, I struggled to assuage my grief. I'd frequently buy two bottles of cheap wine at night—one and a half to dull my senses and put me to sleep. The other half to take the edge off after I woke up in the morning.

Alcohol, among my other idols, was a frequent companion into my late 20s. Even during the first few years of my pastoral ministry, I'd visit the bottle after a *hard* day. On multiple occasions, I'd drink to the point I couldn't remember how I got to bed.

After one particular occasion—frustrated with the way my life was going—I stopped at the liquor store on my way home and bought a bottle of Southern Comfort. I walked into the house, grabbed a glass, filled it with ice and sat down in my recliner. It was already late and the kids were in bed. My wife, without a word, went to bed and left me in the living room with my whiskey and my bad attitude.

The morning after a night like that often led to contemplation time. The negative impact on my body, along with my wife's displeasure vocalized in no uncertain terms, became the backdrop for a conversation with the Lord.

"Son, why do you drink?" I sensed the Lord ask me.

"For comfort after a long or hard day. To calm me down . . . feel good."

"I want you to come to me for those things," He said.

As obvious as it is, it had never really dawned on me that I was looking to a substance for the exact things He had promised to give me. That was the beginning of understanding my idolatry and how it had taken root in my life. This pattern of behavior had started in my teens and had become a stronghold in the season after I lost Julie. It was only later that I realized how.

The Lord helped break my dependence on the counterfeit sources. He taught me how to seek and depend on Him to find everything I needed.

CR8O

Destroying Idols

Here are some practical steps to break away from idols in your life. Start by making a list. Especially as you navigate around the hurts the Lord brings to your attention.

Identify the Idol

What behaviors, substances, or relationships have you used to try to counter the effects of the wounds and lies you've believed about yourself? What else are you looking to for comfort, peace, happiness, or significance?

What has God promised you? Righteousness, peace, joy, love, value, acceptance, and more. So are you turning to anything or anyone else for those things He's given you freely?

Another idol common in the people I've worked with—including myself—is *self*. Because I didn't trust the Lord or anybody else, I depended on me for provision, my perceived righteousness, and my protection. I wouldn't trust anyone, including the Lord, to protect me. So I took it upon myself to judge and screen the people and circumstances in my life through the lens of my wounds, ensuring I wasn't hurt again. Even though my efforts failed miserably and the idol of *self* failed to deliver time and time again, I was still unwilling to make myself vulnerable to others.

Confess Your Idolatry

Because idolatry is a sin, one of the best places to start is to confess it before the Lord and possibly a trusted friend or Christian counselor. Once you've confessed it as sin in agreement with the Lord, receive your forgiveness and your righteousness.

Look for hidden idols in vows and declarations over your life. *I'm never going to trust anyone again. I'm never going to treat my kids that way.* Words like *always* and *never* can usually be traced back to some form of idolatry—because you've made yourself god in that part of your life.

Destroy the Idol

In the same way you break the power of lies in your life, reject and break agreement with the idea that the idol can truly deliver what it promises to give.

Renounce

The idol did provide you something. Acknowledge what it was and take the next step to despise what it gave you—renounce all of its false provision, pleasure, etc.

I can tell you that without exception, anything and everything I turned to as a source other than God has overpromised and under-delivered. The price was always higher than the temporary value I contrived from my idols.

Turn and Receive God as Your Source

As you destroy the idols, reaffirm that you recognize God as the source in that area of your need. Acknowledge that He is your provider and He will supply your every need.

Also, don't hesitate to ask the Holy Spirit to help you transition your focus from the idol to the Lord. He will absolutely answer you. Even on the Sea of Galilee—in a storm, in the middle of the night—Jesus showed us how to rest in the Father's bosom. We have been called to the same place of security in Him. Let the power of these truths resonate within your heart:

- Peace was given to you—it can't be taken away
- The only way your peace leaves is if you allow it to go
- You are in Christ—who is at the right hand of the Father in heaven—like on a sea of glass (no turbulence)
- If you're not experiencing peace, it's because you've turned to an idol instead of the Lord

Cℬⵘ

Chapter 20

The Path Forward

Here are some thoughts to keep in mind as you travel this path. Keep them close and put them to use as often as needed. And as you continue on your way, know that you are amazing. You were created for a purpose—God has a wonderful plan for your life.

Healing from the past is only the first part of the journey. There is a destination for your life. You have a purpose and a destiny. The bulk of this book is dedicated to removing the obstacles that keep you from laying hold of what Christ already has laid hold of for you. Here are some tips and thoughts to help you on your road to full restoration.

ᚳᚱᚨᚮ

F.A.C.T.

This acronym can help you remember the components of restoration:

Faith. Reflect on God's Word. Learning the truth of Scripture and establishing it in your heart are the substance from which your faith and hope are constructed.

Agreement. Agree with the truth regarding who God says you are. Reject and disagree with anything that is not in agreement with the Word of God and His promises to you.

Confession. Let the words of your mouth and meditations of your heart declare the truth of God's Word over your life.

Time. Hold on to the promises the Lord has given you, regardless of the duration of time. Even if you die without receiving the fullness of the promise—hold on! Consider Abraham, Isaac, Jacob, and the examples in Hebrews 11, the hero-of-faith hall of fame. Time builds testimony.

ഗ്ദാ

A Word about Pain

It's going to hurt as you walk out your healing. So expect it. In those painful times, remember that it's only temporary—a normal part of the **healing process.** You can be sure that if the Lord is exposing your pain, it is your **assurance** He is also healing it!

Give yourself permission to feel whatever you need to feel. Your emotions are neither good nor bad, they are what they are. On the other hand, suppressing your emotions can actually hinder the healing process. If you struggle to allow yourself the freedom to express your emotions, ask the Lord for help. There may be some lie preventing you from using this function fully. For example, *men don't cry* is a lie that has kept many men from feeling free to release the pain they carry.

Many times the circumstances or behaviors surrounding pain may contain things that cause a sense of guilt or shame. You don't have to accept or carry either of them. Jesus Christ took your guilt and your shame to the cross. You are free from them.

If the Lord is addressing something that has caused you guilt or shame, know that He is not doing it to condemn or shame you. **Your healing or deliverance is His only motive. No shame—no guilt!**

Feeling Pain Is Not Wrong

You need to know it's okay to feel hurt. You may have been run over by an emotional truck. God isn't mad at you for being hurt—He's concerned for you. He loves you. He died for you.

If your child or loved one walked outside and someone ran them over, what would be your first concern? You would want to make sure they are healthy. And that's what the Lord wants for you.

Re-learning to Trust

During the wounding process, trust is violated—making it difficult to trust anyone. But living a life of distrust is not the solution. I'm not suggesting you put trust in people. That would be a trap.

Thus says the Lord, "Cursed is the man who trusts in mankind and makes flesh his strength, and whose heart turns away from the Lord." (Jeremiah 17:5)

As with most people, I've had many opportunities to learn not to trust people. This verse in Jeremiah was comforting to me—and so I used it as a justification to not trust people. As I grew in the realization that it is impossible to have any relationship without some kind of trust, I inquired of the Lord. One of the first things He showed me was that He didn't say *not* to trust people. What He said was not to *put your trust* in humanity.

There is a huge difference between the two. You can't have a healthy relationship without some level of trust—but you can trust people without putting your trust in them.

Oftentimes we refuse to trust people in order to protect ourselves from pain. But we know that distrust isn't what the Lord has for us because it's motivated by fear. As we place our trust in the Lord, we can extend trust to those around us.

People will hurt you, let you down, and violate your trust. If your trust is in the Lord, then you won't be moved by the inconsistencies of others. It's wise to measure the amount of trust you extend. I like to give people enough trust to start building more trust with me. I'll overextend trust to a degree because that's how it grows. If I encounter someone who isn't trustworthy, I'll measure my trust to the extent I believe it will benefit the other person without violating my own heart.

Because love always believes the best of others, I avoid the idea of writing people off or giving up on relationships. I'm able to exercise wisdom and love, looking for opportunities to build upon what is available without exposing personal information that may not be stewarded in a trustworthy manner.

Even though I endeavor to be at peace and develop trust with everyone, there are some situations where it's not good to do so. In those cases, I intentionally separate myself from those who are unable or unwilling to respect the healthy boundaries I have placed in my life.

As a younger believer, I used to feel guilty separating from some people, thinking I had failed as a Christian. After all, shouldn't Christians love and accept everybody? Maturity combined with wisdom has readjusted my beliefs. I'm responsible for the health of my relationship with the Lord, my wife and family, and myself—first and foremost. If I'm not healthy at the core of my life, I will have nothing of lasting value to give others outside that circle.

Watch over your heart with all diligence, for from it flow the springs of life. (Proverbs 4:23)

I am not responsible to love and accept everyone. I am not responsible for the salvation of everyone. I am not responsible to save or deliver everyone. I am responsible for my own heart. I am responsible to stay away from those things that could damage or impair my heart.

I yield my heart to love those the Lord sends me, and I measure out trust with wisdom. If I sense that someone is unsafe and feel hurt or threatened by them, the first thing I do is look to my own heart. I ask the questions as outlined in this book: Is the Lord using this person to expose something in my own heart? Is this a divine setup to initiate a conversation about some area of my heart that needs healing or maturity?

There are times when it's clear that the relationship isn't going to be healthy for either party. In a few instances, I have completely shut the door to certain relationships with no intention to revisit them unless the Lord so directs me.

I leave it up to you and the Holy Spirit to decide which relationships to build and which to avoid.

ॐ

Recognize Your Own Growth

There is something I often encounter when working with individuals in the healing process. It's the propensity to view ourselves in light of our perceived failures or inadequacies.

As a young pastor, I was in fervent pursuit of a life that honored the Lord in all that I did. When the Lord gave me victory in one area of my life, I'd quickly shift focus to the next area I was struggling in. When I sensed that I was growing strong in an area, I'd look to the next weakness that was staring me in the face. One day, out of the blue, I heard the Lord speak to my heart, "Stop chasing your spiritual carrot!" Then I saw in my mind's eye the picture of a mule with the rider on its back, holding the stick with the carrot dangling in its face.

Regardless of how much effort the mule may have expended, he'd never reach the carrot. Each step forward for the mule was a step forward for the carrot. I understood it was exactly what I'd been doing in my walk with the Lord. With every step forward, I was adjusting the ideal I was reaching for to always be beyond my reach.

It was in that season that the Lord helped me understand that I'm called to live in the present. I'm called to be who I am and enjoy the place He has me in today. If I'm to move, He leads me. But in this moment, regardless of what point I am in the process, I am called to rest and rejoice in the work He is doing in me.

As you're getting free and learning to walk in victory over former sinful or destructive patterns, encourage yourself with the understanding that you are progressing.

CB&O

Progressive Steps of Growth

Helen and I started walking through these dynamics in our relationship. At the beginning stages, we'd get pulled into destructive behaviors like wagon wheels caught in a rut. We felt powerless to change our course regardless of our effort. But by the end of the process, we not only could see what was coming, we had full power to decide how we'd proceed in those situations. So can you.

Step 1: Recognizing Unhealthy Behavior

The first step in transforming behavior is recognizing what things you're doing that aren't healthy. In some areas of your life, you may now be realizing the actions and attitudes you've been engaged in are outside of God's best for you. Don't let that discourage you—it's actually proof you're growing.

If you recognize the need to change, then that's proof you're progressing. It's an affirmation that the Holy Spirit is helping you. Without His help, you wouldn't even be able to recognize that the behavior is outside of His will.

Step 2: Recognizing Your Unhealthy Behavior After-The-Fact
The next step is to realize that what you've engaged in missed the mark. Sometimes you and I can get so entrenched in behaviors that they seem normal at the time. Being able to reflect on those actions and see where the change needs to be is progress.

Step 3: Recognizing Unhealthy Behavior While You're Doing It
As you learn to process new thoughts and beliefs in retrospect, you will begin to recognize when you're getting off track while still engaged in the act itself. Even though it will still seem you're powerless to get back on track, the fact you're recognizing the behavior while doing it is proof you've progressed to the next step in the process of overcoming the behavior.

Step 4: Becoming Aware of Situations That Lead to Unhealthy Behavior Before They Happen
The final phase of victory is when you're able to anticipate situations and circumstances that have previously provoked that reaction in you. You'll be able to prepare for, or in some cases, avoid those situations altogether.

∞

It's very easy to find the areas that still need work. But it takes training and intention to look for the things that are going well. You can teach yourself to see what God is doing in your life and celebrate your progress.

Because you're already completely forgiven and fully pleasing to the Lord, there is no need to excuse or justify the areas of your life that still need help. Neither do you need to become prideful or arrogant when you succeed. You will continue to move forward with the strength God gives you. Take time to recognize your growth and celebrate each step you take. Encourage yourself in the journey.

CB80

Be Encouraged:
Never Give Up

"I am so proud of you." That is what I hear the Lord saying to you.

Because I've been actively applying the concepts in this book for the last two decades, I know the courage it takes to walk this path. The challenge it takes to forgive those who have hurt you. The searing pain of opening wounds in your heart that have been hidden away for years. The feeling of burning tears that have been held back for far too long.

Even though I can never fully identify with your pain, I can certainly relate to it. And because of that, I am proud of you.

It is my sincere hope and prayer that these thoughts, examples, and tools have and will help you find freedom. Freedom from anything that would hinder you from experiencing everything available to you in Christ. Freedom to walk in the fruit of the Spirit. I pray they help you as they have helped me.

I've walked through many deeply painful encounters with the Lord as He helped me apply His provision to those wounded areas of my heart. In those places, I've learned what I've shared with you in this book.

But I've also discovered that these tools aren't limited to the deep, dark painful areas of life. They are useful in the day-to-day bumps and bruises of life as well. I regularly find myself applying the same steps to everyday circumstances. When my flesh is displaying itself, I guide myself through the same progression I've shared with you.

I've found that I'm still not living my life in full agreement with my identity in Christ. Like Paul, I am pressing on to that mark. When I encounter an obstacle, I pause and take the time to bring it through the process of acknowledging it, forgiving those involved, taking ownership of my responses, and then inviting the Holy Spirit into my thoughts, feelings, and behavior. As the Lord shows me what is beneath my responses, I confess, repent, receive both my forgiveness and my righteousness, then move forward in agreement with Him.

At times I find there are still issues that need the extra time and attention to dig deep. Most times, I can address them on the fly.

My point is simply this: Don't expect a quick fix or a one-and-done-type encounter. If your desire is to continue to grow in Christ, then expect this to take time and process. There is healing for each area of your heart and mind. But just like a person who is run over by a truck, there will be multiple issues that need to be addressed. The ones that are life threatening must be addressed first. Recovery—and subsequently, the maturation process—will take time. Additionally, there may be areas of your life and relationships that will need rehabilitation.

There have been instances, even within the last six months of my life, where the Lord has had me revisit certain beliefs about myself that were rooted in events of my youth. My initial response was, "Are you kidding me? When am I going to be completely free of this stuff?"

To be real with you, I was discouraged. Then something happened. I sensed the Lord encourage me to look back at where I came from. I have come so far. He has done so much. I have so much peace, joy, and victory in my life. I have so much freedom. So one more time I set my heart to walk through the process for myself. As always, I was so glad that I did.

* * *

Loved ones, this will take some time. Be encouraged. Everything the Lord brings to the surface is for your freedom. It's for your healing—like the dross brought to the surface of gold, only to be swept away. Each time you walk through this process, it will bring you another step forward to what is rightfully yours: freedom, wholeness, peace, and joy.

Your God loves you so much. His desire is that you walk in fullness of joy. He wants you to experience life, love, and true freedom. He is completely committed to the process of leading you through—not around—the obstacles that attempt to prevent you from having it all.

The price has been paid. It's yours and it's available to you. **Rise up and take it.**

In those times when the pain is most severe, don't give up. Hold on to His promise and press through. There is hope—never doubt that. There is nothing in your life, nothing you've done, and nothing that has been done to you that is bigger than God's love for you. He has already proven His love and commitment to you by sending Jesus Christ, His Son, to die for you. He is ready, willing and able to lead you into the abundant life that is already yours in Him.

For I am confident of this very thing, that He who began a good work in you will perfect it until the day of Christ Jesus. (Philippians 1:6)

CR&O

MEET THE AUTHOR

As an ordained minister in the body of Christ, Luke Laffin has been training and equipping believers for over three decades. He has authored articles and international missions devotionals, developed Bible-based curriculum, and maintains a blog on his website: www.lukelaffin.com.

His first book—*Reclaiming Your Core: Restoring the Foundations of Faith*—delivers a foundational and transformational insight into the gospel and received such favorable reviews as "pure gold, well-balanced with real truth, grace, and love." His second book—*Go Face Yourself: A Healing Journey*—takes the reader on an insightful, life-promoting journey to process the pain from past wounds and re-emerge victorious in Christ.

Over the years, Luke's career has been prolific—working as an international speaker, author, teacher, life coach, as well as a business owner and professional consultant.

He has developed and led ministry teams nationally and internationally, counseling and training many individuals throughout the years. Now in his 50s, he works alongside his wife, Helen, pouring into others the lessons they've learned through many heartaches, joys, challenges, victories, and failures.

In 2014, Luke and Helen founded Four Winds Global Foundation to help others discover their true identity, purpose, and passion in Christ. He and his wife also work with leaders to navigate the pressures and challenges of marriage, family, and ministry.

As much as possible, Luke and Helen spend time with their children and grandchildren living in various parts of the country. They also pursue a healthy lifestyle and enjoy working out together—completing two Spartan Race events since turning 50.

APPENDIX

Wound Identification Worksheet

Helps identify and clarify potential areas that may need healing.

1. Describe current events, circumstances, or relational dynamics causing emotional pain, frustration, anger, fear or anxiety:

2. Describe a situation in which your response doesn't reflect the fruit of the Spirit (love, peace, kindness, etc.):

3. Clearly identify the emotions you are feeling beneath your actions:

4. If you are experiencing anger, what feelings or concerns are at the heart of the anger?

5. Does the situation you are thinking about remind you of other similar events in the past? If so, please describe:

6. Who were the people involved?

7. What did you feel in that moment?

8. What did you believe about the people involved or what they represent?

9. What did you believe about yourself?

10. What vows, conclusions, or judgments did you make?

Anatomy of a Wound Worksheet

Helps you discover the impact each wound has had.

1. State the nature and details of the wound:

2. When was the first time you felt pain associated with this wound?

3. What did you believe about yourself?

4. What conclusions did you make about others?

5. Did you make any vows, promises, or decisions as a result of this event? How have these choices impacted your life and/or relationships?

Discovering Your Wounds Worksheet

Helps you uncover more about your wounds.

1. **Painful memories.** What memories cause pain or evoke sorrow, regret, or other types of pain?

2. **Off-limit topics.** What topics do you (or those in your relationships) avoid? Include any thoughts of why you believe that is the case:

3. **People you avoid.** Identify the people you avoid and note any details of why you avoid them. Is it because of past or current issues? Is it because you're uncomfortable around them or do they remind you of someone who makes you feel uncomfortable?

4. **Physical pain associated with emotions.** Do you experience painful responses to emotional situations? Describe the situations, emotions, and details of the pain. What type of pain is it and where is it located?

5. **Cyclical patterns.** Do you find yourself in the same type of relationships or situations? Do you feel that certain outcomes are predictable in your life? Describe them here. Consider the situations where you use terms like always or never.

6. **Disproportionate emotional responses.** Are there times where you find yourself reacting in ways that exceed what others deem appropriate? Describe the dynamics of those situations here. Are there common themes either in your response or in whatever is provoking your response?

7. **Controlling behavior or unrealistic fears.** Do you feel insecure, frightened, or angry with certain people or in certain situations if you aren't in control? Do you have unrealistic fears or phobias causing you to avoid people or things?

8. **Areas of self-preservation.** Describe any areas where you go out of your way to protect yourself. Are there certain people or situations you intentionally avoid in order to protect yourself from being hurt or taken advantage of?

What is the Truth about Me?

Our old programming. How I think/feel about myself. I renounce the lie that . . .	What is true about me: What God's Word says about me. I declare the truth that in Christ . . .
I am unlovable.	**I AM VERY LOVED.** John 15:9; Rom. 8:35-39; Eph. 2:4-6; 1 John 3:1a, 4:10
I am unacceptable. I am unworthy.	**I AM ACCEPTED.** John 15:15-16; Eph. 1:3-6 **I AM RIGHTEOUS.** Rom. 8:31-34; 1 Cor. 6:19-20; 2 Cor. 5:21
I am inadequate. I am a failure. I am fearful.	**I AM ADEQUATE.** 2 Cor. 2:14; 3:5-6; 12:9; Phil. 4:13 **I AM VICTORIOUS.** Rom. 8:37; 2 Cor. 2:14; 1 John 5:4 **I AM FREE FROM FEAR.** Ps. 4:8; 27:1; 32:7; 2 Tim. 1:7; I John 4:18
I am anxious. I am weak. I am not very smart or good enough.	**I AM CONTENT.** Ps. 4:8; 37:5; Phil.4:6-7, 11; Heb. 13:5; 1 Pet. 5:7 **I AM STRONG IN CHRIST.** Acts 1:8; 2 Cor. 12:9-1O; Eph. 1:19; 3:16; Phil. 4:13 **I HAVE GOD'S WISDOM.** John 15:15; 16:13-14; 1 Cor. 1:30; James 1:5; 1John 2:20-21, 27
I am in bondage.	**I AM FREE.** John 8:32, 36; 2 Cor. 3:17; Gal. 5:1, 13a

I am unwanted and belong to no one.	**I'VE BEEN ADOPTED BY GOD; I AM HIS CHILD.** Rom. 8:16, 17; Gal.4:5-7; 1 John 3:2
I feel guilty.	**I AM TOTALLY FORGIVEN.** Eph. 1:7; 2:13; Col. 1:14
I am depressed.	**I HAVE THE JOY OF THE LORD.** John 15:11; 17:13; Rom. 15:13; 1 John 1:4
There is nothing special about me.	**I HAVE BEEN CHOSEN, SET APART BY GOD.** John 15:16; 1 Cor. 1:30; 6:11; 1 Peter 2:9 **I AM A TEMPLE WHERE THE HOLY SPIRIT DWELLS.** 1 Cor. 6:19; 2 Tim. 1:14
I am hopeless.	**I HAVE ALL THE HOPE I NEED.** Rom. 8:20-25; 15:4, 13; Col. 1:26-27; 1 Peter 1:3
I feel condemned.	**I AM BLAMELESS.** John 3:18; 5:24; Rom. 8:1
I am alone.	**I AM NEVER ALONE.** Rom. 8:38-39; Heb. 13:5
I can't reach God.	**I HAVE ACCESS TO GOD—ANYTIME.** Eph. 2:18; Heb. 4:14-16: 1 Peter 2:5, 9; 1 John 5:14-15
I am afraid of satan. I have no confidence.	**I HAVE AUTHORITY OVER SATAN.** Col. 1:13; 1 John 4:4; Rev. 12:7-11 **I HAVE ALL THE CONFIDENCE I NEED.** Prov. 3:26; 14:26; 28:1; Eph. 3:12; Phil. 1:6; Heb. 10:19; 1 John 5:14

Adapted from writings of Neil T. Anderson. Used by permission.